"Come, you novel readers, and lay aside your farm ~~~ narratives, your theological thrillers, your second-coming serials, and pick up the gripping tale of Antipas—historical fiction, empire-wide, martyr-deep, too true not to have happened. But beware the power of this story's addiction. Do not begin this book unless you are willing to be putty in the storyteller's hands, for he will force you to take up residence in an old world, about to be reborn in the blood of good souls. No fiction these souls! Real they are, and their reality will cause you to cry out to them, 'Adelphos-Brother! I had to see you die, so I might learn to live.'"

—Calvin Miller, Beeson Divinity School

"A savvy and creative introduction to the New Testament world, disguised as a collection of 'lost' letters between Luke and several well-positioned members of Roman society. The genius of the book lies in its fusion of current New Testament scholarship with a very plausible, personal narrative: the sobering story of one man's shift in allegiance from Caesar to Jesus. Along the way we overhear pagan reactions to Jesus' message and endearing stories from household churches; we sense the perils of sea travel and witness the horrors of the Roman games; we identify with privileged benefactors and hurt for subsistence farmers. Anyone hunting for a reliable, if not always comfortable, guide to the dangerous world of first-century Roman Christianity should be glad these papers were finally 'discovered.'"

—Bruce Fisk, Westmont College

"This fictional correspondence is not true, but it certainly could have been. Longenecker writes a very engaging account of several characters who, in their different ways, came to experience and respond to the risen Jesus Christ through Luke's narrative. I was especially moved by the character of Antipas as he is ennobled by being transformed from a Roman dignitary into a model of Christian self-sacrifice."

—Stanley E. Porter, president, McMaster Divinity College

THE LOST
LETTERS OF
PERGAMUM

A STORY FROM THE
NEW TESTAMENT WORLD

BRUCE W.
LONGENECKER

WITH EXTRACTS FROM
BEN WITHERINGTON III

Baker Academic
Grand Rapids, Michigan

© 2003 by Bruce W. Longenecker

Published by Baker Academic
a division of Baker Publishing Group
P.O. Box 6287, Grand Rapids, MI 49516-6287
www.bakeracademic.com

Seventh printing, December 2008

Printed in the United States of America

Library of Congress Cataloging-in-Publication Data
Longenecker, Bruce W.
    The lost letters of Pergamum : a story from the New Testament world / Bruce W. Longenecker with extracts from Ben Witherington III
        p.   cm.
    ISBN 10: 0-8010-2607-5 (pbk.)
    ISBN 978-0-8010-2607-2 (pbk.)
    1. Luke, Saint—Fiction. 2. Church history—Primitive and early church, ca. 30–600—Fiction. 3. Bible. N.T.—History of Biblical events—Fiction. 4. Evangelists (Bible)—Fiction. 5. Christian saints—Fiction. 6. Physicians—Fiction. I. Witherington, Ben, 1951– II. Title.
PS3612.O53L47 2003
813'.6—dc21   2002074407

For our son Callum:
May the narrative of your life
be marked out by honor

CONTENTS

AUTHOR'S PREFACE

Antipas, my faithful witness, . . . was put to death in your city [Pergamum]—
where Satan lives.

Revelation 2:13

The narrative of the final year of Antipas' life that appears in the following pages is fictional. It arises from one supposition, one fact, and one tradition. The supposition is simple: that the Antipas mentioned in Revelation 2:13 had been named after Herod Antipas, the son of Herod the Great and pro-Roman tetrarch who reigned over Galilee during the time of Jesus' ministry. The fact is equally simple: that this Antipas died as a martyr for Christ in Pergamum (cf. Rev. 2:13), where pro-Roman sentiment and emperor worship were rampant. Add the supposition to the fact, and a proto-narrative emerges of one who began life dedicated to the advancement of Rome and ended his life as one perceived to be an enemy of Rome. Add to this the ancient tradition about Antipas' gruesome martyrdom (see below), and the narrative virtually writes itself. A storyteller need only fill in the blanks. In doing precisely this, I found that the narrative often had as much control over me as I had over it.

Some of the constraints that the narrative imposed on me were the socio-economic, political, and religious dynamics of the time in which the narrative is set. While the narrative is largely informed by imagination, it is my hope that my imagination has been well informed by reliable study of the historical period and the ancient culture in which the narrative is immersed. When browsing through bookshops, it is not unusual to find novels whose story line is set in the ancient world. These have great appeal. All too often, however, their authors demonstrate little knowledge of the social codes and implicit structures that animated the ancient world. In these novels, a modern story line is simply wrapped in the façade of antiquity by giving the characters ancient names, placing them in ancient cities, giving them ancient

9

clothes and means of transport, and feeding them ancient foods. From a historical point of view, such narratives are disappointing, whatever their literary merit. What such novels often lack is an appreciation for the dynamics that drove ancient cultures. My hope is that readers of this narrative will not only enjoy the story line for its own sake (despite its somewhat grisly details at times) but will also profit from a better appreciation of the historical context of the early Christian writings and, thereby, develop sharper instincts for understanding the writings of the New Testament in their contexts. The reader will no doubt emerge better informed after reading the snippets of information that appear along the way in the narrative, many of which have been cobbled from Ben Witherington's accessible book *New Testament History* (Grand Rapids: Baker Academic, 2001). The real aim of this narrative, however, is to "enlighten by means of ethos" as much as by information so that readers might "experience" the realities of that world in a manner that narrative is so well suited to foster.

The narrative that unfolds in the letters that follow is fictional, but it is not unrealistic. To elaborate, I have fond childhood memories of being told stories or watching plays that took place long ago and far away. On several of these occasions, I remember asking my mother afterward, "Did that really happen?" To this she regularly gave the answer, "No, but it could have." I acted satisfied, as if my little mind clearly understood what she meant. But her answer was puzzling and confusing and has stayed with me (for that reason, perhaps) ever since. I remember thinking on more than one occasion, "If it *could* have happened, how does she know that it *didn't* happen?" But my mother has always been wise, and I believe there was wisdom even in this enigmatic saying. What she was getting at, I suspect, was a twofold truth: First, the story itself could not claim to be a "true story" that was based on actual events; second, the story was "true to life" and did justice to the historical setting in which it was placed. If that interpretation of her words has merit, then let the reader of the following narrative understand that, while the story did not happen, it could have happened.

Since this is a work that intermingles "fact" (so called) and fiction, it must be noted that the fictional character of the narrative begins with the introduction of the "editor" in the editor's preface. Just as the editor is fictional, so too is the pretext of the discovery of this ancient correspondence. At the end of the book, an appendix includes brief indications as to which aspects of the narrative are fictional and which are based on reliable historical reconstruction (appendix C). It is placed at the end so as not to distract attention from the narrative itself. I have not attempted to document all the sources on which the historical reconstructions are based; readers wanting such documentation may refer to Witherington's *New Testament History*. For the most part, the historical reconstructions contained in this book are in harmony with the reconstructions in that book.

The ancient philosopher Aristotle once wrote, "The perfect friendship is that between good men, alike in their virtue." The following narrative explores some of the dynamics of friendship, goodness, virtue, and honor in the ancient world of the Roman empire, in which Jesus and his first followers proclaimed the message of a different empire ("the empire of God") and enacted distinctive forms of friendship, goodness, virtue, and honor.

Bruce W. Longenecker

EDITOR'S PREFACE:
THE DISCOVERY

Let us now praise famous men.

Sirach 44:1

I t wasn't until we opened the casements and began to probe their contents that we realized the full extent of the discovery we had stumbled upon. Entombed within those casements, hidden from human eyes for nearly two thousand years, lay the fragile but miraculously preserved literary remains of famous men. The ancient city of Pergamum had generously given up one of its last remaining secrets, and I had been the beneficiary of its generosity.

The discovery was itself a corporate find. In the last two decades of the twentieth century, archaeologists from Germany, the United States, and Turkey took a keen interest in excavating the ancient site of Pergamum. Previous excavations of the ancient city had already uncovered some of its remains, but there was much more to do. The task of recovering this important site from the rubble that had overtaken it became urgent in view of the increasing pressures of modern construction developments that threaten to engulf the ancient remains. Visitors to the site of Pergamum (in the modern city of Bergama toward the west of Turkey) will today witness the encroachment of modern buildings upon all areas of the ancient city. This is most noticeable with regard to the ancient amphitheater, the theater, and the Sanctuary of Asklepios, the last of which is now strangled by military bases. It became imperative to study the accessible remains of the ancient city before they too became inaccessible to modern probing. With these concerns in mind, I joined the archaeological teams already in place, bringing with me a small team of archaeologists sponsored by my university.

In the course of our excavations, the remains of ancient temples and civic centers of various kinds were unearthed, along with a variety of ancient houses. When excavating one of these houses, my team discovered three lead casements that had purposefully been stored away. The casements had long ago been sealed with pitch and wax, placed within a recessed space between the remains of two stone-wall partitions, and entombed within a low-grade concrete casing. Most of the concrete casing was undamaged, except for one corner that had fallen away. Two of the casements had survived the passage of time unscathed; one casement showed signs of damage, but only slightly so. (The damage to it was due to the fact that it protruded from the gap in the concrete casing, possibly caused by an earthquake tremor.) Ultrasound explorations of the casements revealed what appeared to be documents. Experts in papyri and parchment manuscripts were given the task of extracting and examining the documents. Although fragile, those documents proved to be enormously resilient against the effects of time and emerged from their makeshift tombs virtually intact. In only a handful of insignificant places has there been need to postulate what the original text might have been.

The first English translation of these intriguing ancient documents appears in the following pages. The collection involves an exchange between well-placed and influential persons based in both Pergamum and Ephesus. In the ancient world, scribes frequently made copies of private correspondence prior to the delivery of the original documents to their intended recipients. The parchment documents discovered at Pergamum appear to include copies of Pergamene letters sent to Ephesian residents in some cases, and in other cases the original Ephesian letters sent to Pergamene residents. The one who long ago placed the letters in their protective casements, therefore, appears to have been a resident of Pergamum. These documents were clearly treasured by their long-deceased owner, who at some point gathered them together and stored them to keep them safe and perhaps (in light of some of their contents) to keep himself safe.

The primary figures in the exchange are (1) Antipas in Pergamum, an elite pro-Roman businessman, and (2) Luke in Ephesus, an important figure in early Christianity whose two-volume work (the Gospel of Luke and the Book of Acts) comprises over one-quarter of the New Testament. Although we know something about Luke from his writings contained in the canon of the Christian church, almost nothing has previously been known about Antipas, who comes to life through these letters as a figure of great interest.

Since a few of the extant letters are dated according to day and month, we know that the exchange takes place over a period of ten or so months (mid-January to early October), with several indicators in the letters suggesting that they were written in the year 92 C.E. In the majority of cases in which specific dates are not mentioned, I have provided estimates in footnotes as to the date of each letter. Readers who choose to disregard these footnotes will not be at a disadvantage in understanding the basic unfolding of events. But the estimates may benefit those interested in precise chronological sequence.

It has not been possible to discern the identity of the house in which the lead casements were discovered. In all likelihood, it was the house of Antonius (who plays a large role in the narrative conveyed by the letters), although this is impossible to verify, and other explanations might also be possible.

Three additional items of explanation are required. The first concerns editorial notes. I have occasionally included footnotes to explain the historical setting and context that the letter writers themselves take for granted. I have also included within the letters bracketed comments to explain small features with which the general reader may be unfamiliar or literary references assumed by the letter writers. Also on occasion I have prefaced the letters with brief editorial notes containing observations that should be read in advance of reading the correspondence or indicating the section of Luke's Gospel that Antipas has read and is discussing in the letter that follows. For fullest effect, it might be helpful for readers of the correspondence to familiarize themselves with the relevant passage from Luke's Gospel prior to Antipas' discussion of it.

Second, maps identifying the main locations discussed in the narrative follow the postscript (appendix A). I have also devised a list of characters (appendix B). Readers are encouraged to consult the list as needed.

Third, the delivery of private letters between cities was a burdensome task in the ancient world. Private letters were frequently delivered by entrusted travelers on the route or by commissioned servants. The delivery route between Pergamum and Ephesus could be covered by land in four days (some eighty miles, at twenty miles per day, or more for a fit messenger). A reply would require the help of travelers journeying in the opposite direction or, as in the case of this correspondence, the return journey of the commissioned servant. At places in this correspondence, Luke's response to one of Antipas' letters could not have been delivered until Antipas' servant made a subsequent round-trip, delivering Antipas' next letter to Luke and then returning again to Antipas. Therefore, a staggered effect needs to be taken into account when dating some of the letters. In my translation, however, I have ordered the letters according to their content rather than their strict chronological sequence so that Antipas' letters are followed immediately by the relevant response from Luke, regardless of how much later those responses might have been written.

Sometimes chance encounters between people start out as inconsequential but become life changing. If a chance encounter brought Luke and Antipas together, these letters indicate that such an encounter did not remain inconsequential for long. Neither should it remain Pergamum's secret any longer.

The Editor

To the angel of the church in Pergamum write:
"These are the words of him who has the sharp, double-edged sword. I know where you live—where Satan has his throne. Yet you remain true to my name. You did not renounce your faith in me, even in the days of Antipas, my faithful witness, who was put to death in your city—where Satan lives."

Revelation 2:12–13

AS ONE
NOBLEMAN
TO ANOTHER

Antipas' Letter

Antipas,[1] son of the nobleman Philip, civic benefactor of the cities of Tyre and Caesarea, freeborn citizen of the blessed empire of Rome, and worshiper of Jupiter, Zeus Olympios the Savior;

To the most excellent Calpurnius, son of the distinguished Theophilus, benefactor of the people of Ephesus, nobleman of the Lydian region;

Greetings.

On this tenth day before the ides of January [5 January], I write to you, most excellent Calpurnius, as one nobleman to another, with an invitation from L. Cuspius Pactumeius Rufinus, a leading official of the city of Pergamum and one to whom I have committed myself. Rufinus has managed to earn from our great emperor Domitian the honor of sponsoring two days of gladiatorial contests in the course of the next year. As you may have heard, Rufinus' father, Drusus, has recently died and has left an endowment along with instructions for sponsoring two gladiatorial days in Pergamum. These instructions are being implemented by Rufinus himself, who will use the occasion to celebrate the memory of his father as an esteemed citizen of the empire, as well as to celebrate our beneficent gods and our illustrious emperor, whose guiding spirit fills the empire.

The first gladiatorial day will take place on the thirteenth day before the calends of April [19 March; the "calends" is the first of the month]. The second will fall just before the autumn equinox on the sixteenth day before the calends of Domitianus [15 September].[2] These days will adorn the great city of Pergamum, whose citizens are even now full of anticipation.

---

1. As in most ancient correspondence, the sender (i.e., Antipas) is identified first in the letter, and the addressee (i.e., Calpurnius) is identified second.

2. At this time, Domitian had renamed the months of September and October "Germanicus" and "Domitianus," respectively. The traditional names were reinstated after Domitian's death.

19

Rufinus has conscripted me to undertake several organizational tasks for these gladiatorial contests, which I am happy to do. One of those tasks includes extending an invitation to the honorable men of the region, bidding them to attend and thereby helping to promote harmony among the great benefactors of our regional cities. Since you rank among that esteemed number, it falls to me to request your presence at the first of these occasions. You would be one of six officially recognized representatives of the noblemen of Ephesus, Pergamum's sister city in concord and itself a promoter of Rome's magnificence. You will have a place specially reserved in the *tribunal editoris* [the area designated for highly regarded civic magistrates alongside the holder of the contest], together with the other noblemen and invited guests. Although the emperor has agreed to offer part of his own gladiatorial troupe for the occasions, he himself will not be in attendance. Nonetheless, many esteemed citizens will be gathered, and we hope that you will be among that number. Should you and your entourage require housing for the event, I have a list of Pergamene noblemen who will gladly extend hospitality to visiting noblemen. Simply let me know your needs, and I will make the necessary arrangements.

The gladiatorial school here at Pergamum is making preparations for the event, and we have notified the gladiatorial schools in Smyrna and Philadelphia as well, each of which have agreed to supply contestants for the first event. Gladiators from Galatia and Egyptian Alexandria will also be there. At present just over one hundred gladiators have been purchased for the day, but Rufinus is hopeful for more. If you meet with any itinerant *lanistae* [owners of gladiatorial troupes] who are not aware of these events, we would be in your debt if you would pass on the information. They should make contact with Rufinus of Pergamum directly.

Euphemos of Pergamum, my honorable host, also sends his greetings. Stachys, my servant, delivers this message. If your response to this message is not delayed, he is at your service for delivering your response to me. He should be no burden upon you. I have instructed him to find accommodation at a local inn if you require him to remain overnight before delivering your response.

May the gods continue to bless you and your household.

Calpurnius' Letter

Calpurnius of Ephesus, son of Theophilus;

To Antipas, nobleman of Pergamum;

Greetings.

You have honored me with your kind request for my attendance at the gladiatorial contest in the spring. The occasion falls just prior to a voyage that I hope to make, so I should be able to attend. I am not a keen enthusiast for the contests, you should know, since throwing men to wild beasts or watching them kill each other in combat for the amusement of spectators has never seemed to me either prudent or tasteful. But your invitation is gracious, and I am concerned to preserve healthy relationships between the cities of Ephesus and Pergamum. Their long-standing competition for civic honors and prestige has too frequently induced an unhealthy enmity between the noblemen of our two grand cities. While I applaud civic competition to the extent that it sharpens our interest in promoting the beneficence of our own citizens, I regret the lack of concord that occasionally transpires. For that reason, although I will not revel in the contests, I nonetheless consider it my civic duty to comply with your gracious invitation and represent my fair city in the Pergamene games. The riot that broke out between the people of Pompeii and Nuceria at a gladiatorial competition some thirty years ago clearly indicates the severity with which Rome looks upon intercity discord, with the emperor forbidding further shows in Pompeii for a decade and rewarding the senator who sponsored the competition with exile. There is a need for intercity cooperation in events of this sort, and so I will be content to play a role in ensuring civic stability. I am greatly honored by your invitation. I

21

will make my own housing arrangements for the time that I am there, since I have strong ties with certain leading men of Pergamum.

Your host, Euphemos, is himself a man of high repute, and your association with him in Pergamum is sure to prosper. Please send him my regards.

Your servant Stachys has been no burden. Upon my insistence, he was provided with food and accommodation at my own house. I did not want to subject him to one of the crude local inns that are famous for their bedbugs and foul practices. I send him back to you with a gift of friendship for you, along with this brief letter.

Farewell.[3]

---

3. If Antipas wrote his letter on 5 January, his messenger Stachys would have departed from Pergamum on 6 January and arrived in Ephesus on the afternoon of 9 January. If Stachys then left Ephesus on 10 January, he would have arrived back in Pergamum on 13 January with Calpurnius' reply.

A PERSONAL
REQUEST

Antipas' Letter

Antipas, benefactor of cities of the empire and student of great literature;

To the most excellent Calpurnius, nobleman of Ephesus and protector of the library of Theophilus;

Greetings.

Rufinus was pleased to hear of your intention to attend the first gladiatorial contests that he will sponsor this year in Pergamum. Your presence will honor us. Your views about the necessity of promoting intercity harmony among the elite are especially appropriate and fall well within Rufinus' expectations for the day. I am certain that your astute influence will be felt within the amphitheater.

I have noted, honorable friend, your hesitation about gladiatorial combats in general. I am aware of similar concerns offered by some philosophers, many of whom the emperor Domitian has now banished from Rome. They denounce gladiatorial contests as a profane practice that brings infamy and shame upon our society, eroding the character of our citizens and degrading our humanity.

Those are important views to keep in mind lest we become bestial in our thirst for blood, like the roguish barbarians who threaten the extremities of our great empire. We should not be dominated by an interest in bloodletting, as they are. But it seems to me that philosophers who hold critical views of the competitions do not give enough credence to the fact that many of the victims at gladiatorial games are themselves representatives of the underbelly of society: highway robbers, butchering murderers, treasonous villains, escaped slaves, and foreign prisoners of war. These people are deserving of their end. Moreover, to die in the contests gives them the chance to meet their deaths in a heroic fashion, bringing some honor to their shamed name. And as long as they survive the contests, they are provided with food and lodging at their master's expense. Some gladiatorial survivors even become objects of adulation and affection among the women, and great gladiators occasionally find their reward in being granted freedom. So the gladiators themselves can benefit from their profession in a number of ways.

So too can the spectators. The competitions provide ample entertainment for our citizens, including the peasantry, who otherwise have very little to enjoy or look forward to. It is only the specter of public shows of one sort or another that breaks the monotony of their relentless concerns about grain supplies and economic hardship. Moreover, the gladiators exemplify for the spectators the noble attributes of Rome herself: courageous bravery, dogged endurance, and overpowering might. The wild-beast hunts in a gladiatorial event parade a host of exotic creatures drawn from all over the empire, highlighting the empire's magnificence and reinforcing the narratives on which our society is founded—the triumph of virtuous and orderly civilization over the forces of lawless barbarism and primeval chaos. This is why so many amphitheaters throughout the empire are built between a city and the vast regions surrounding it, pinpointing the location where civility meets barbarism. Now that Rome has mightily established stability and peace throughout the world, the savage desire to conquer that lies within the soul of humanity is temporarily assuaged in the extravagant gladiatorial displays of unrelenting power and force. Were it not for the gladiatorial contests, the savagery of the barbarians might again rise up to engulf societal harmony.

In my view, then, gladiatorial games bring benefits to society that far outweigh any of their more unattractive aspects. Of course, when judged from one angle, gladiatorial combat may appear distasteful, but there are other angles that place it in a far more acceptable light. It is my hope that you will be able to enjoy the gladiatorial contests by considering them in that light.

My primary purpose in writing again to you is not to burden you with arguments about the merits of the contests, for it would be presumptuous of me to think that you are unaware of them. Instead, I write with a personal request. Although I am now a man of leisure, I remain proud of my academic prowess and continue to acquire the same amount of pleasure from reading and study as I do from entertainment and sport. Euphemos, my host, has recounted to me the magnificence of your personal library, a treasure of repute from Macedonian Philippi to Egyptian Alexandria. I am currently in pursuit of the Alexandrian edition of Homer. Both his *Iliad* and his *Odyssey* are preeminent classics of the Hellenistic storytellers, and I have an interest in studying sections of the Alexandrian edition of Homer in particular. The splendid library here in the Pergamene temple of Athena holds an edition of Homer established by the Pergamene librarian Crates, but this edition appears to be different from the edition I studied years ago with an Egyptian philosopher while living in Caesarea. I have made arrangements with new friends here in Pergamum to spend some weekly leisure time comparing the two editions. I am hopeful that your magnificent library might hold an Alexandrian edition of Homer and that I might gain access to that edition (or perhaps to sections of it) by your kindness. Stachys, my servant, will deliver my donation for your efforts in this regard and as a guarantee for the safe return of your manuscripts of Homer by the time the rains end in the spring.

Euphemos himself had intended to write you regarding this matter, but I preferred to do so myself, since I am relatively new to Pergamum and need every opportunity to establish myself with men of honor in the region. While a businessman, I owned extensive tracts of land in the rural regions of Galilee, where I maintained and augmented the fortune of my long-established lineage. Although most of my landholdings were in Galilee, I spent most of my life as a respected citizen in the magnificent cities of Tyre and then Caesarea Maritima, on the eastern coast of the Mediterranean Sea. I have maintained my honorable status through civic benefaction in these cities, including the installation of ornate pavements, fountains, baths, and statues.

My desire to enjoy the leisure of study in my advanced years has brought me to Pergamum. Fifteen years ago, I read the first few volumes of Pliny's newly published *Historia Naturalis*. Since then, I have remembered his description of Pergamum as "by far the most distinguished city in Asia" [*Hist. Nat.* 5.30]. And so, now that I have the opportunity, I have come to enjoy the pleasures of this distinguished city—"the citadel"[1] in the heartland of imperial Asia. I have been impressed by Pergamum's remarkable position, seated at the top of a conical outcrop high above the surrounding valley. To match its impressive location, it is comprised of the most spectacular sacred and royal buildings, not least the great altar of

---

1. The name "Pergamum" means "citadel."

Zeus, whom we now know as Jupiter. The gods are worshiped in abundance here, including of course the divine emperor Domitian and the savior Asklepios, the god who heals us from our afflictions.

Another attraction of this fine city is its exceptional collection of books. From my previous travels, I have gained extensive knowledge of many of the empire's libraries, and I imagine only the libraries in Athens and Alexandria to rival the Pergamene collections. There are also many book collectors in this city with a variety of literary artifacts. So my enjoyment of life here in Pergamum will be enhanced by the luxury of contemplation on the higher things of life. Already I have engaged in profitable discussion of Aischylos, Sophocles, and Euripides with some local connoisseurs of the literary classics, and I look forward in the future to studying a good number of historical texts. At present, however, the Homeric collection is of primary interest. If you were able to send me an Alexandrian version of the master's works, I would be significantly in your debt.

I (along with my servants) will continue to be resident in the house of Euphemos for the foreseeable future, by his kindness. If this request is in keeping with your pleasure, your copy of Homer will also become a resident at good Euphemos' house.

May the gods be gracious to you and your household.

CALPURNIUS' LETTER

Calpurnius of Ephesus, son of Theophilus;

To Antipas, nobleman and friend;

Greetings.

It is my pleasure to send the Alexandrian edition of Homer to you, by way of your servant Stachys. This is one of the prized possessions in the library of Theophilus, my father recently deceased. As a bibliophile, my father wanted his books to be shared with others, so I am content to send you the manuscripts that you are seeking. Your scribes may copy them while they are in your possession.

Since you are new to the area, you might be interested to know about a close associate of my household, an esteemed doctor and scholar named Luke. He is currently in Troas, where he has been instructing Eutychus, a friend. Since the shipping lanes have closed for the winter, he will return to Ephesus by land, passing through Pergamum on his return journey. He intends to stay as a guest in the house of Antonius, a city magistrate and man of great repute. Luke shares with you a keen interest in history. Before his death, my father, Theophilus, commissioned Luke to write a historical account of an intriguing man from Galilee and his followers. Luke finished this historical monograph about ten years ago. Despite its length (it extends to two sizable volumes), it remains in great demand. No doubt you and he would have much to discuss with regard to recent events in and around Galilee. Perhaps Antonius could let you know when Luke arrives in Pergamum, since you both would profit from each other's interests.

I have kept your servant Stachys for longer than you might have wished; he faced a difficult storm on the way here and, despite his insistence to the contrary, was in need of recovery. He is indeed a strong and fit messenger, for few would have emerged from the fierce storm as well as he has. Since it was by my insistence that he stayed, perhaps you will not be too harsh with him. I have sent with him some spices from Arabia in case I have wronged you in any way by this course of action.

If you find other gaps in the Pergamene library, do not hesitate to make contact again.

Farewell.[2]

---

2. Speculative dates for this correspondence might be as follows: Stachys departs from Pergamum on the morning of 20 January, arriving in Ephesus on the afternoon of 23 January; Stachys leaves Ephesus on the morning of 27 January, carrying Calpurnius' reply and arriving in Pergamum on 30 January.

TO HONOR
THE EMPEROR

Antipas' Letter

Antipas, citizen of the Roman empire, nobleman of Pergamum, benefactor of many;

To Calpurnius, gracious nobleman of Ephesus and esteemed friend;

Greetings.

It was with the greatest of regret that I was unable to meet with your associate Luke, who passed through Pergamum earlier in the week. Being somewhat new to the city, I felt it necessary to attend a banquet sponsored by Julius Quadratus, a most illustrious man, a leading city official and benefactor of the Pergamene people, as you may know. Having recently returned from visiting Rome, Quadratus held a banquet to celebrate the establishment of a new Pergamene temple to Apollo and Asklepios, son of Apollo. Having been invited to the banquet, I was obliged to attend and was pleased to do so. I did, however, take the occasion of the banquet to praise you before Quadratus as a man of honor in our neighboring city of Ephesus. Quadratus already knew of your father's reputation, as well as your own. I look forward to meeting Luke on another occasion if he is to pass through Pergamum at a future date.

By your kindness, the Alexandrian edition of Homer arrived at the house of Euphemos and is now in my temporary care. I have been studying the Pergamene and Alexandrian editions along with my esteemed friend Euphemos and others who gather occasionally in his house. We have noted differences between the Pergamene edition compiled by Crates and the Alexandrian edition compiled by Aristarchos. For instance, at one point both versions include the phrase "The Okeanos,[1] genesis for

1. "Okeanos" (cf. "ocean") is the great salt-water sea of ancient mythology.

all" [Homer, *Iliad* 14.246]. In the Pergamene edition, this is supplemented with an additional phrase, so that in Crates' view the entire passage should read: "The Okeanos, genesis for all men and gods, and it flows over the whole earth." Crates is well known for having challenged the traditional view that the earth is a flat disk floating on water, advocating instead a spherical earth covered in large measure by water. It seems likely that Crates' idiosyncratic view has influenced his editing of Homer at precisely this point.

I would be pleased if you could make provision for my servant Stachys once again. I have instructed him to be no trouble to your household. (He is an exceptional messenger, preferring to make quicker time by traveling alone rather than being accompanied by another. The dangers of his travels are consequently increased, of course, but as you can tell, he is well able to protect himself from most perils.) He brings with him a large flask of olive oil in return for your graciousness. Your previous permission for him to recuperate within your house was most kind and posed no complications to my own arrangements. (Having relocated in Pergamum, I now have need of only eight servants, whom I keep busy with the organizing of my local affairs: a bursar, a steward, two scribes, a doctor, two personal servants, and Stachys, my messenger. Upon leaving Caesarea, I turned the rest of my household over to my eldest son, Androneikos, who continues to live in Caesarea while overseeing the businesses based in Galilee. Androneikos, overseeing a household of fifty-five servants, prospers there as much as my forefathers and I did.)

I have given instructions ensuring that, after he departs your house, Stachys should deliver on my behalf a substantial contribution to the construction of the new imperial baths and gymnasium currently under construction in Ephesus, your magnificent city. As a Roman citizen, I regularly seek to promote the empire of Domitian—the earthly regent of Jupiter, the mighty god, Zeus Olympios. I have made similar contributions in several other cities. Even in Pergamum, I have already funded the construction of an impressive street statue to honor the emperor. It will be erected prior to the spring gladiatorial contest and will be clearly visible upon entering the city. It should be a welcome sight to any who come to Pergamum to worship the emperor at the great citadel of the gods. The background of the statue will be the imposing specter of the Pergamene acropolis. Ephesus' recent honor of becoming a temple warden to the cult of the emperor[2] [89 C.E.] puts it in the same league as Pergamum, itself the first city of Asia to establish a temple to a Roman emperor over a century ago. So I seek to honor Ephesus and its loyal citizens with this gift, just as the emperor himself contributed to the recent improvements to the Ephesian temple of Artemis, including a statue in honor of himself.

May Jupiter, the most high god, look favorably on you.

---

2. The term "temple warden" *(neokoros)* was applied to those cities that had been granted permission by Rome to establish temples for the purposes of emperor worship. Those distinguished cities served as custodians of the imperial cult in their region.

LUKE'S LETTER

Luke, doctor, historian, and servant of God;

To Antipas, man of honor, scholar, benefactor;

Greetings.

I write with unfortunate news about Calpurnius of Ephesus, with whom you have been in recent contact and whose household I am now helping to oversee. Calpurnius has left Ephesus quite unexpectedly and by great necessity. He is now traveling by land to the seaport city of Patara, where his brother Philoneikos is a civic officer. Philoneikos has just lost his firstborn, a son of twelve years, whose cheeks, in the flower of youth, bloomed with a thin down. Calpurnius intends to deliver his condolences personally to his brother, whose heart is downcast. Calpurnius will stay for as long as his presence is beneficial. If that should be for a month or more, the shipping lanes will be open again, and he will proceed on the journey to which he has long been looking forward. He is likely to purchase passage on one of the first ships to Caesarea, a city that has prospered from your own benefaction. (The northern winds will ensure speed for the journey, although the seas will still be threatening. I pray for his safety.) From there, he will travel to his destination, Jerusalem, to see what remains of the temple that used to stand there and to imagine the city as it might have been before being shattered by the Roman forces in the Judean revolt [66–70 C.E.]. I expect Calpurnius to return to Ephesus in time to enjoy the summer months with us. In the meantime, I am helping to manage his household.

Along with this letter you will find a note of apology from Calpurnius' own hand, explaining that he will no longer be able to attend the

Pergamene gladiatorial contests this spring and requesting that another Ephesian nobleman be invited in his place [this note has since been lost].

Calpurnius will be glad to hear that the Alexandrian edition of Homer is being put to good use by you and your colleagues. His father, Theophilus, considered it his duty to make his book collection widely available to promote knowledge in the region.

By the way, I have recently come across an opinion on Homer held by the prolific Jewish historian and apologist Flavius Josephus. In one monograph, Josephus speaks of Homer's narrative as being "preserved by memory and assembled later. . . . And it is because of this that there are so many inconsistencies in it" [Josephus, *C. Ap.* 1.13]. You may want to be alert, then, to narratival inconsistencies as you study the Pergamene and Alexandrian versions of Homer.

I see from the scribal copy of Calpurnius' earlier letter that you have been informed about the historical monograph that Theophilus commissioned me to write. I have taken the liberty of sending with Stachys a freshly transcribed copy of the first volume of that monograph, in case it is of interest to you. This first volume [Luke's Gospel] recounts the life of Jesus of Nazareth, a Galilean who was crucified when Pontius Pilate was governor of Judea. With your strong connections to Galilee, Antipas, you may find this narrative to be of interest, so I entrust it to your care. Many of us who call ourselves Christians believe this Jesus to be the Jewish messiah, or Christ, and the human incarnation of the most high God. I would only ask that, were your scribes to make a copy, they would do so with extra vigilance and care, since I would regret variant traditions of the narrative being promulgated in the same way that variant editions of Homer have been promulgated. Copies of the monograph are continually being made for Christians around the Mediterranean basin, but Calpurnius' scribes are busy with the management of the household and cannot produce them as quickly as we would wish. I myself have overseen the production of this copy and therefore verify its authenticity.

It was unfortunate that Quadratus' banquet coincided with my passing through Pergamum on my way back to Ephesus. (Antonius, my Pergamene host and friend, was also to attend that banquet but unfortunately was prevented from doing so due to a temporary illness.) Perhaps we will have occasion to meet at some point in the future. You and your servants are always welcome in Calpurnius' house.

I, Luke, now write this with my own hand.[3] I was pleased to welcome
Stachys, who has proven to be your faithful servant in helping to estab-
lish a favorable friendship between the house of Calpurnius and yourself.
Grace be to you.[4]

---

3. A change in handwriting is evident at this point, confirming that the letter had been dictated by Luke to a scribe. Here Luke picks up the writing implement and adds his own farewell.

4. Dating this set of correspondence is informed by Luke's reply to Antipas. Luke mentions
that Calpurnius might spend a month in Patara before boarding one of the first ships to Caesarea. Shipping lanes were generally closed from mid-November until mid-March (although
the safest months to sail were between mid-May and mid-September). This places Luke's letter just after mid-February 92 c.e. Speculative dates for this correspondence might be as follows: Antipas writes his letter prior to 15 February; Stachys departs from Pergamum on the
morning of 15 February, arriving in Ephesus on the afternoon of 18 February; on the morning
of 19 February, Stachys delivers the contribution to the Domitian bath-gymnasium. He probably spends an additional night in Calpurnius' house and then leaves Ephesus on 20 February,
arriving in Pergamum with Luke's letter on 23 February. This means that Antipas and his colleagues had studied Homer for approximately two weeks before sending word of their findings
to Calpurnius' household.

THEY PROCLAIM
A DIFFERENT
LORD

Euphemos and Antipas' Letter

Euphemos of Pergamum and Antipas of Tyre and Caesarea, benefactors of the people and loyal subjects of the emperor;

To Luke of the house of Calpurnius in Ephesus, scholar, historian, friend;

Greetings.

Euphemos and Antipas have the pleasure of presenting Lysanius Paullus of Miletus with a celebratory offering on the occasion of his appointment as regional Asiarch [promoter of the imperial cult]. We would be in your debt, friend, if you made provisions for our servants Domnos and Kuseron in their travels through Ephesus to and from Miletus. A small gesture of thanks accompanies this request.

May the gods be gracious to you.

Luke,[1] I must thank you for your helpful letter. Euphemos and I wonder, however, whether you might be somewhat uncomfortable in your association with Christians. Their reputation throughout the empire is suspect. If our understanding is correct, they proclaim a different lord than the emperor and promote a different empire than that of Rome. They frequently stir up trouble and have the blame for ravaging Rome, the imperial city, with fire [64 C.E.]. Certainly your association with them does not enhance your honor. Please excuse our frankness of speech; you are clearly worthy of being treated as a friend, and so we speak boldly on this matter.

1. The letter from Euphemos and Antipas to Luke begins as a typical letter of general recommendation, with Antipas' own comments added to the bottom of the letter.

Your monograph about the god of the Christians will no doubt be of interest. I am afraid we have not been able to study it yet; it arrived only a few days ago. How very impressive it looks!

The older I get, the more I am aware of the speed with which time passes. The spring gladiatorial contests are soon upon us. Preparations for this one-day event are on course, and we are expecting a fine occasion, with approximately 130 gladiators now enlisted for the afternoon combat alone. Of course, the Pergamene amphitheater does not have the infrastructure to support the kind of extravaganzas that are so popular in the great Flavian amphitheater of Rome [known later as "the Colosseum," which was opened by the emperor Titus of the Flavian dynasty in 80 C.E.]. For instance, we will not even attempt to orchestrate the water battles in which condemned men reconstruct great sea battles as the means of their execution. Filling the basin of the amphitheater with water would itself involve a tremendous feat of engineering, and the workforce and material resources required would increase the cost of the event substantially. But although the Pergamene contests will not be on the same scale as the emperor's extravagant shows in Rome, the attractions will still have a high entertainment value.

I will send Stachys to you with the return of the Alexandrian edition of Homer in the near future. My scribes are now copying it for deposit in the libraries of Pergamum.

May you continue to prosper.

LUKE'S LETTER

Luke, follower of Jesus Christ, friend of Antipas and Euphemos;

To Antipas, esteemed benefactor and patron of the people, and Euphemos, revered citizen and nobleman;

Greetings.

It has been my pleasure to welcome your servants Domnos and Kuseron into the house of Calpurnius. They spent a day here before beginning the second half of their journey to Miletus and have returned here on their way back to you. Because they have walked for eight continuous days since I last saw them, I insisted that they remain here for a day before undertaking the final leg back to Pergamum. Your gifts of provision are received with thanks. I will ensure that Calpurnius hears of your kindness.

I am convinced that the lack of water battles will not detract from the reputation of Rufinus' Pergamene contests. After all, not everyone is as thrilled by the water battles as the emperor Domitian. His recent exploits with water battles have drawn further attention to his severe temperament, unlike that of his father, Vespasian [Flavian emperor 69–79 C.E.] and his brother Titus [Flavian emperor 79–81 C.E.]. You will know, no doubt, that he famously fashioned a lake out of dry land near the Tiber River and sponsored a water spectacle there. The report of that event has come to me from various sources. Evidently, after the battle commenced, the rains began to fall heavily, pounding down upon the spectators. The emperor covered himself and changed clothes to heavy woolen cloaks but forbade the people themselves to take any precautions against the rains. As a result, a number of local residents fell ill and later died. On this occasion, at least, the emperor revealed himself to be more concerned with promoting his own well-being than with the welfare of his subjects. The

we Christians worship is known to have forsaken his own interests and
well-being in order to serve the welfare of his worshipers. The society that
he promotes is one that brings health and wholeness to all.

For this reason, although I am grateful for your concern about my own
notoriety with regard to my association with Christians, I assure you that
I find no dishonor in being a Christian. I am able to document the point
more clearly in my two-volume monograph on Jesus of Nazareth and his
followers, if you care to consult that work. The reputation of Christians
as antisocial miscreants is undeserved and based on misinformation, as I
seek to explain in that narrative.

Regarding the Christians' involvement in the burning of Rome,
although that was Emperor Nero's official view, his version of events is
not well founded. If blame is to be placed, many people, even senators
in Rome, now suspect that the blame for the burning rests on one man
alone: Emperor Nero [emperor 54–68 C.E.].[2] This is impossible to verify,
of course, and it is most likely that the fire simply started by accident.
But if the fire was, in fact, started by Nero, such an action would not
be out of character for him. A variety of sources indicate that Nero had
been inclined to vice, especially in the later years of his reign when he was
known to have indulged all his excesses. This was evident in his official
dealings but also in his unofficial lifestyle—prowling disguised through
the streets of Rome at night, indulging in sexual debauchery with women
and boys, and picking fights with men. One incident reveals the extent
to which he was willing to sacrifice the honor and life of others to protect
himself. I have heard that one evening, while in disguise on the streets of
Rome, he began a fight with Montanus, one of his senators whom he happened to find along the way. Montanus fought back but then made the
fatal mistake of apologizing for his blows. This signaled to the emperor
that Montanus had recognized him. With his own reputation at risk,
Nero forced Montanus to commit suicide. In the aftermath, whenever
Nero took to the streets in nighttime revelry, he took guardsmen with him
so that they could finish the fights for him in a similar manner, thereby
preventing the risk of being detected.

I must also note that, in his recent historical monograph *Jewish Antiquities,* Josephus records a remark that the praetorian tribune Subrius

2. Suetonius (c. 66–122 C.E.) and Dio Cassius (c. 155–235 C.E.) both concluded that the
fire was an act of wanton destruction by Nero (Suetonius, *The Life of Nero* 38; Dio Cassius,
History of Rome 62.16–18).

Flavus allegedly made to Nero [65 C.E.]: "I began to hate you after you murdered your mother and your wife, and became a charioteer, and an actor and an arsonist" [Josephus, *Ant.* 15.67]. The first three of these four charges can be shown to have validity, and possibly the fourth should fall into the same category. The first charge of murdering his mother and wife is not disputed. Having exercised considerable influence over Nero in the early years of his reign, his mother, Agrippina, later made the mistake of criticizing his mistress, Poppaea Sabina, and was promptly executed [59 C.E.]. Octavia, his wife, was the next to be executed, thereby permitting him to marry Poppaea.

The second charge of becoming a charioteer is likely a reference to the occasion when he crowned Tiridates as king of Armenia. During the ceremony of the crowning, Nero somewhat inappropriately took the opportunity to give a public performance on the lyre, after which he donned full charioteer regalia and drove a chariot around the arena while the crowds watched. Such unruly and undisciplined behavior was ignoble and ill-suited for one on whom the destiny of the empire depended.

The third charge of being an actor refers to his love of the arts, especially late in his reign. He is known, of course, to have plundered the great art treasures of Asia for his own palace [61 C.E.]. On one occasion he attended the Isthmian games in Corinth to recite his poetry and sing. He established an arts festival in Rome in his own honor. On the second occasion of this festival [65 C.E.], he took the stage himself. Although he gave a clearly second-rate performance, his senators thought it best to shower him with embarrassed praise, awarding him with crowns for singing and for oratory at the expense of the other competitors.

So the first three of Subrius Flavus' charges against Nero can be substantiated. Consequently, the fourth charge, that he was an arsonist, may well be accurate also, if the fire was not simply accidental. And if Nero did have something to do with the fire, then Subrius Flavus' third and fourth charges might be intricately connected. It was Nero's aesthetic sensibilities that led him to announce his desire to rebuild Rome in a more artistically pleasing style, and it was this desire that would have resulted in his drunken burning of the city in order to allow for its rebuilding.

From what I have been able to reconstruct, the fire that devastated large portions of the city was no ordinary blaze. It lasted for six days [19–25 July 64 C.E.], followed by a brief hiatus, followed then by three further days of blaze. Three of the fourteen regions of Rome were completely leveled, and only four regions escaped without damage. The fire initially began near the Circus Maximus and spread north along the Palatine, destroying shops, homes, and temples in the very heart of the city. What increases suspicion about Nero's culpability is that this was precisely the area he wanted to rebuild as a new city in his honor, to be called Neropolis. In the aftermath of the fire, the heart of the razed area was the place that Nero chose as the location for his "Golden House"—his extravagant imperial palace with its own manmade ornamental lake and a colossal statue of Nero himself.

After the fire, in view of the suspicion regarding imperial arson, Nero found a convenient scapegoat in the Christians. As punishment against them, Nero clothed some of the Christians in skins of wild animals and set loose dogs on them, which promptly tore them to pieces. Some were crucified as enemies of the state, and others were used as living torches to light his nighttime circus games. The communities of Christians in Rome were dealt a devastating blow, enduring torturous deaths with nobility out of loyalty to their savior, Jesus Christ, and never failing to stand firm for their way of life. I have had it reported to me that two of the greatest ambassadors of the Christian way of life, Peter of Capernaum (who appears in the two volumes of my monograph) and Paul of Tarsus (who appears in the second volume), were martyred in the senseless slaughter initiated by Nero. I knew both men personally, especially Paul, a Roman citizen with whom I traveled for some time. The character of these men was above reproach. But of them I would have much to say, and I have already gone on for too long in response to your query.

My point is simply that Nero's charges against the Christians regarding the burning of Rome are almost certainly without foundation, and so too were the severe recriminations against them. In fact, in my monograph on Jesus the Galilean, I demonstrate that he is not one to stir up antisocial behavior within society. Indeed, he is one who brought health to society, redefining the codes of honor and instigating a way of life that replicates the values of the highest God of goodness. In the second volume, I am able to demonstrate that being a Christian does not conflict with being a responsible citizen, as long as the processes of the empire do not erode into chaos. No doubt you, as an honorable citizen and benefactor of the good, might be interested in studying the life of Jesus of Nazareth precisely to assess my argument for yourself.

I have received word that Calpurnius has stayed in Patara and is await-ing spring passage on a ship to Caesarea, as he had hoped. I had already sent word to him about some household matters and mentioned our con-tinuing correspondence. He enjoined me to send you his sincere greet-ings, and he looks forward to familiarizing himself with the city that you made your own. From there he will travel eastward to Jerusalem.

May the God of goodness go before you.[3]

3. Speculative dates for this correspondence might be as follows: Domnos and Kuseron depart from Pergamum on the morning of 25 February carrying the letter from Euphemos and Antipas (see Antipas' statement that Luke's monograph has recently been received and my pre-vious suggestion [see the third letter collection] that Stachys returned to Pergamum with that monograph on 23 February); Domnos and Kuseron arrive in Ephesus on the afternoon of 28 February, staying for one day; they depart for Miletus on the morning of 2 March, traveling there and back in eight days; they arrive in Ephesus on their return journey on 9 March, stay-ing for one day; they leave Ephesus for Pergamum on the morning of 11 March, arriving in Pergamum on 14 March (cf. Antipas' statement in his next letter [written around 11 March] that Domnos and Kuseron have not yet returned from their journey).

THE
REPUTATIONS
OF THREE MEN

Antipas' Letter

[The text discussed is Luke 1–2.]

Antipas, benefactor of Tyre and Caesarea and honorable citizen of Rome;

To Luke, esteemed historian and friend;

Greetings.

Along with this letter, Stachys will return to your care the copy of the Alexandrian edition of Homer that Calpurnius kindly loaned to me. I promised to have it back in Theophilus' library by the end of the rainy season and have been true to my word. I have benefited greatly from the opportunity to study it, and my new friends and I have enjoyed many pleasant conversations about the subject matter. The deposit that I sent to secure this text need not be returned to me; please dispose of it in such a manner that promotes Calpurnius' civic honor among the Ephesians.

I benefited greatly from your short explanation of the fire of Rome, and I have taken the liberty to have a copy made and deposited with the library in the Athena sanctuary. If you wish, I will withdraw it from circulation, although there is nothing politically sensitive in what you have written. Rufinus shares your interpretation of the burning of Rome, thinking it either to have been accidental or masterminded by a crazed Nero. Many here in Pergamum believe Nero still to be alive, despite the overwhelming reports that he committed suicide with the help of his freeman [9 June 68 C.E.]. Some imagine that Nero has fled beyond the Euphrates River and is sheltered in Parthia, from which he will return, leading a magnificent army to reclaim his throne, establishing himself as the claimant to the divine throne once and for all. You will know, of course, of the celebrated false returns of Nero. Not long after his reported death, an impostor claiming to be Nero impressed many of the disenfranchised

51

chised in Greece who urged him to reclaim his throne. A decade later, a second impostor appeared in Asia, persuading many that, as Nero, he was the rightful emperor. Even the king of Parthia supported this man in his ineffectual efforts to take the imperial throne. I also know of a third who recently made similar claims in Parthia. Each one has either met his death or been delivered to Rome. So the legend of Nero lives on to this day. I have also heard some compare Nero to Domitian, our blessed emperor. Each has displayed an uncompromising grip over the whole of the empire, removing their rivals with severity.

With regard to your report about Domitian's actions at the gladiatorial contests near the Tiber, I suspect that the rumor about his callousness is overblown, exaggerated by disgruntled peasants wanting to malign the emperor's character. The rumor is perhaps styled on stories of Caligula's actions half a century ago when, during his own gladiatorial contests, he ordered the canopies to be removed in the heat of the midday sun and forbade anyone to leave. But even if the reports about Domitian's actions are true, they must not be unfairly divorced from his actions after the contests, when he demonstrated goodwill to his subjects by providing many of them with a succulent banquet throughout the night. The storehouses of our divine emperor's grace and goodwill are plentiful, since his empire is blessed.

On several occasions now you have made mention of a Jewish historian Josephus. Is he a reliable guide to historical matters? If so, I should be interested in reading his work sometime. At present, however, it is with great pleasure that I, together with Rufinus, have begun to study your own impressive historical monograph on the Jewish peasant Jesus. We have thus far been able to read only the beginning of the narrative, concerning the birth of Jesus, but you have grabbed our attention from the start. We noted with special interest your technique of introducing the Galilean peasant by placing him firmly within the broad and grand currents of Roman history [1:5; 2:1–2; 3:1], rather than simply relating his story within the unsophisticated, rustic context of village life. Rufinus thought you were intending to indicate the significance of your seemingly insignificant main protagonist, whose humble origins are offset by the way in which he subsequently shaped the events of world history, as your prologue so boldly and imaginatively suggests [1:1–4]. Like Jesus, many of the characters in the narrative of his birth seem inconsequential over against the likes of Caesar Augustus, Quirinius, Herod the Great, the emperor Tiberius, Pontius Pilate, Herod Antipas, Herod Philip, and Lysanias, all of whom you mention early on.

One thing also caught our interest in particular: the way in which the Jewish characters seem so easily to slip into tirades against Rome. The otherwise charming Mary speaks of her god as one who "has brought down rulers from their thrones and has lifted up the humble" [1:52]. This is dangerous, clearly. More dangerous still are the words of Zechariah, who speaks of his god granting "salvation from our enemies and from the hand of all who hate us . . . to rescue us from the hand of our enemies" [1:71, 74]. Why do so many Jews see Rome as an enemy? As a priest in the Jerusalem temple, Zechariah might have been involved in offering sacrifices to the Jewish god twice a day on behalf of the emperor Augustus and should have been cognizant of the way in which Rome's almighty rule benefits the whole of the civilized world.

This disturbing tendency to overlook the merits of Rome in favor of a crazed notion of independence reminded us of the recent Jewish revolt against Roman sovereignty, futilely waged in Judea two and a half decades ago. Having to coordinate an army of fifty thousand in order to maintain the peace and security of the Judean area, Rome has rightly taken proper precautions to ensure against further attempts to overthrow its all-powerful reign, decimating the Jewish holy city and temple. Many of the Judeans were seized and forced to compete in gladiatorial contests, where they met their deserved death. Scoundrels the world over must learn that opposition to the eternal rule of Rome is futile.

Rufinus was glad to hear from me that not all Jews in the region surrounding Jerusalem are as hotheaded as those who participated in the Jewish revolt. The Galilean city of Sepphoris, about four miles from the hometown of Jesus of Nazareth, is a case in point. Herod Antipas settled most of its predominantly Jewish inhabitants in that city in view of their pro-Roman attitudes. The city had been destroyed earlier by a Roman governor of Syria upon hearing that a Galilean named Judas had initiated an anti-Roman revolt and had taken control of the city [about 6 C.E.]. In order to demonstrate Roman sovereignty, the governor ordered two thousand Jews to be crucified in Jerusalem. At the time of the widespread Jewish revolt some years later [66–70 C.E.], some of the ten thousand inhabitants of Sepphoris were eager for hostilities against Rome. Most, however, continued to maintain a pro-Roman posture. Those favoring compliance with Rome eventually firmly established Sepphoris as a pro-Roman city without peer. (Those with whom I had business dealings tended to favor compliance, I am pleased to say.) Roman garrisons were welcomed to be stationed there. While the revolt against Rome was underway in Jerusalem, Sepphoris minted its own pro-Roman coins on which it honored Roman leaders and declared itself a city of peace [68 C.E.]. It later dismantled its fortress to indicate its lack of aggressive interests. I assume, since you speak of him as one worthy of honor, that Jesus of Nazareth may have prefigured this cooperative pro-Roman attitude adopted by the majority of his Sepphorian neighbors.

I am pleased to announce that everything is in order in preparation for the Pergamene gladiatorial contest. My scribes have joined with the scribes of Euphemos and Rufinus to advertise the event, describing the forthcoming contest in vivid colors along walls and gravestones in the surrounding area. Perhaps you will also spread the word among your Ephesian colleagues.

I am happy to report that those who enter the city of Pergamum from now on will be welcomed with the sight of an impressive marble statue of our emperor. I myself commissioned this statue for the good pleasure of all the local residents and those who travel here. Three days ago it was unveiled in a grand ceremony and procession, with most local dignitaries participating in the occasion and enjoying a fine banquet that I hosted in the imperial temple. This was my first act of public benefaction officially recognized among the Pergamenes, and I am pleased by the way it has been received. Perhaps good reports will make their way to Ephesus in due course.

I again need to express my appreciation to you for housing our servants Domnos and Kuseron on their travel to Miletus. They have not yet returned to us; I suspect they may be guests in the house of Calpurnius while I write these lines.

Stachys brings a gift in thanks for your hospitality.

I have prayed to Neptune, god of the sea, for Calpurnius' safety in travel, and to Asklepios for your continued health. For the benefit of us all, I have prayed to the divine emperor Domitian, Jupiter's chosen representative and vicegerent, who rules over the earthly sphere from Rome just as Jupiter rules over the cosmos from Mount Olympus.

LUKE'S LETTER

Luke, in the household of Calpurnius;

To Antipas, nobleman and friend, and to Rufinus, preeminent citizen;

Greetings.

Our flourishing affiliation through correspondence pleases me greatly. Your faithfulness in reporting to me on matters of historical and contemporary interest is a source of refreshment and testifies to your own breadth of learning. In your letter to me, you raised points concerning the reputations of three men: Jesus, Domitian, and Josephus. I consider it my duty to reply to those points, however briefly, since I must permit Stachys, your trusted servant, to depart in the morning.

Concerning Jesus of Nazareth, as you read more of my monograph you will find that he would not have been in complete accord with the pro-Roman sympathizers with whom you had business dealings in Sepphoris. Much of what Jesus taught should be welcomed by Rome as a corrective to destructive forces within our society. But the seeds of scrutiny and challenge are also in his message, and I believe that any who neglect it, regardless of their stature, do so to the detriment of themselves and others. I need not say more, since my monograph is available to you.

Concerning Domitian, I appreciated hearing your report about the banquet he hosted at the completion of the gladiatorial contests near the Tiber. The full inventory of that infamous event should indeed be circulated. I am not one who seeks to peddle half-truths as if they were the whole truth. And yet, despite your corrective note, Domitian's conduct at gladiatorial contests remains dubious. You might have heard one report, for instance, about an observer of a gladiatorial contest in Rome who thought it sporting to chide the emperor publicly for his strident preference for *myrmillones* over Thracian gladiators [two types of gladiators]. That man, himself a Roman citizen, was ejected from his seat and shamefully paraded around the arena before being torn to pieces by the arena dogs at Domitian's command. Reports exemplifying the emperor's generosity begin to lose their effectiveness against the sheer number of reports illustrating his cruelty.

I too have heard comparisons of Domitian and Nero. Like Nero, Domitian has great flair for building and refurbishing and has established a lavish palace for himself in Rome. His building campaigns are paid for by heavy taxation imposed in the provinces, including a poll tax on Jews that has been so stringently enforced that many Jews have been taken to court for not paying promptly. Like Nero, Domitian revels in self-glorification, expecting to be addressed as "lord and god" by even the most highly placed senators. Like Nero, Domitian has adorned himself with the graces of culture, writing poetry and instituting quadrennial Olympic games in Rome, complete with chariot races, athletics, and literature contests. He frequently attends these games in Greek dress wearing a golden crown and has the judges wear crowns with his image placed alongside those of Rome's gods. Like Nero, Domitian demonstrates a cold and calculating cruelty toward any that he considers a threat. You will know that recently he executed a provincial governor of Asia and the governor of Britain for supposed treasonous acts [89 C.E.], although their infractions were relatively trivial. He has banished philosophers from Rome for their denunciations of him, killing the two rhetoricians who were most vocal in their protestations against his tyranny. His severity extends even to those who pose no political threat to him. When three vestal virgins were found to have lovers, the lovers were banished and the vestals were executed, the emperor showing clemency by allowing them to choose their mode of execution. The same courtesy was not extended to the head vestal when she also was caught with a lover; Domitian had her buried alive and her lover beaten to death with rods. His severity is renowned, as was Nero's late in his reign.

Concerning Josephus, he is a Jewish historian who has written voluminous amounts on points of historical interest. Most recently he has produced what is likely to be his definitive work on what he calls the *Jewish Antiquities*. The monograph is extensive, amounting to twenty volumes of detailed study of Jewish history from ancient times until today. So clearly, he is a most impressive historian. Much of his work is driven by an apologetic agenda, of course, so it cannot always be taken at face

value. For instance, one of his major works is entitled *Jewish War,* a monograph written fifteen years ago or so. It seems to have been written as a
propaganda piece. In it, he tries to dissuade other Jews from rising up
against Rome [Josephus, *J. W.* 3.108] and to protect the Jewish religion
from an antisocial reputation in the aftermath of the Judean uprising
against Rome. For instance, Josephus deliberately downplays the role of
the Pharisees in the uprising, hoping to protect them, for they were the
faction of Judaism with which he has been most closely associated. At one
point in his life he even sought to become a member of their party [Jose-
phus, *Life* 11–21]. In general, Josephus consistently casts blame for the
Jewish war against Rome on a few hotheads who were able to whip up
the Jews into an unnatural and exceptional fervor.

This itself is curious, since Josephus was himself a general in the Jewish forces against Rome. As the Roman general Vespasian took his troops
to invade Galilee, many Jewish revolutionaries fled in advance of his coming. Josephus took refuge in the city of Tiberias and then moved on to
Jotapata, which the Romans eventually surrounded for several weeks.
Although most of the men were captured and executed, Josephus managed to escape and went into hiding in a cave. Vespasian's forces eventually discovered his whereabouts, and Vespasian planned to send Josephus
to Nero for trial. But at this point Josephus played the role of a Jewish
prophet, predicting that not only Vespasian but also his son Titus would
become Roman emperors. The Jews had, in Josephus' view, misinterpreted
their own ancient scriptures, expecting the long-awaited anointed one to
be a Jewish messiah who would lead them out of Roman oppression, just
as the Hebrews had been led by Moses out of Egyptian bondage into
national freedom. According to Josephus, the long-awaited anointed was,
in fact, a Roman military general, Vespasian, soon to rise to rule as emperor.
As a result of these favorable predictions, Josephus was retained as an aide
within Vespasian's forces. When Vespasian returned to Rome to take up
the mantle of emperor [69 C.E.], Josephus was taken along with Vespasian's
entourage. It helped Vespasian's legitimacy in Rome to have an adversar-
ial warlord acting as a divine oracle in his favor. News of Josephus' prediction spread throughout Rome. He was given residence in the imperial
household and vast tracts of land in Judea free from imperial taxation.

Since settling in Rome, Josephus has set about writing historical mono-
graphs on Jewish history. I noted with interest his attempt in *War* to balance his belief in the sovereignty of the Jewish God with the reality of

Roman rule. He suggests that the God of Israel has granted world sovereignty to Rome for a while but has not, in fact, been defeated by the gods
of Rome. The God of Israel is permitting Rome a period of reign prior
to the time when Israel's God will once again rule over creation without
intermediary.

You will forgive my musings on these issues. The sun has long set, and
I am alone with my scribe Zosimos, eager to send a report back to you
with Stachys. Until his next visit to Ephesus, I will look forward to your
further correspondence.

We too pray for Calpurnius' safety in travel and for each other, in the
name of Jesus Christ our Lord.[1]

1. Antipas' reference in his letter to having returned the manuscript of Homer before the
end of the rainy season, along with indications from earlier letters, permits some speculative
dates for this correspondence: Antipas writes the letter prior to 11 March; Stachys departs from
Pergamum on the morning of 11 March, arriving in Ephesus on the afternoon of 14 March;
Stachys leaves Ephesus for Pergamum on the morning of 15 March, carrying Luke's reply, and
arriving in Pergamum on 18 March.

JESUS SEEMS
A CURIOUS
FIGURE

ANTIPAS' LETTER

[The text discussed is Luke 3–4.]

Antipas, benefactor of the people and citizen of Rome;

To Luke, scholar and friend;

Greetings.

It is my great pleasure to report what you are likely to have heard already: The Pergamene gladiatorial contests were a great success. Rufinus has drawn up his own report on the day, which has been deposited in the city archives. Copies of his report have been made for wide circulation. One copy has been sent to the emperor himself, who provided some gladiators from his own troupe. I have several copies at my own disposal and enclose one of them with this letter, imagining that it might be a record of interest even within the Ephesian archives.

As you will see, the spectators were offered a feast of amusement and entertainment in grand fashion. As the sponsor of the day, Rufinus has received high praise and adulation from local residents, as well as the leading men of Pergamum and the neighboring cities. His reputation is held in increasingly high regard. My own part in assisting with the organization of the contests was publicly recognized by Rufinus, who in his banquet speech after the contests made mention of me and his other associate, Kalandion, showering us with praise, accolades, and gifts.

Your information about the historian Josephus came as a tremendous surprise. I had heard much about him while resident in Tyre during the time of the Jewish revolt, before relocating to Caesarea. Word spread like wildfire about the capture of the general of the Jewish forces in Galilee who preserved his life by ingratiating himself with his Roman overlords.

I remember that he was kept in Caesarea for the majority of the war, but once Vespasian departed for Rome, I heard no more about him, except that many Jews continue to speak ill of him, imagining him to be a traitor. Who would have imagined that a general of an unfortunate troupe of Jewish rebels would rise to become a great historian of Jewish antiquity in the household of the almighty Roman emperor. His god must indeed look favorably upon him. I look forward to enjoying his writings after studying your own monograph.

I greatly regret that our discussions of your portrait of the Nazarene Jesus have been hindered recently. This is due to a combination of factors, not least the post-competition affairs and responsibilities and the heavy rains that have been unkind to my health. But after a two-week hiatus, Rufinus and I met outside the city walls in the temple of Isis, the mistress of Pergamum, to continue our reading and discussion of your narrative.

During our discussion, I chanced upon an idea of some interest to me. Following our consideration of your text in the forthcoming weeks, I will strive to recount to you the issues we discuss arising from your monograph; if you should find it good to respond to our impressions, so much the better. The opportunity to discuss a significant piece of historical writing with its author is rare and holds great interest for me. (Who would not jump at the chance to discuss Homer's texts with Homer himself!) So perhaps you will permit me this luxury. If the gods permit, I will seek on a regular basis to send to you a brief synopsis of our discussion. If you care to reply to any point, that would be welcome, certainly, although I cannot conscript you into an enterprise of my own devising. Perhaps this suggestion is the product of an aging mind. If you find the suggestion unattractive in any way, you will of course let me know.

Even though we read only a brief section of your monograph, we were both impressed with your compositional skill. I must confess, however, that the lineage of Jesus [3:23–38] did not assist us in clearly locating Jesus' heritage, since almost all the names you mentioned are unfamiliar to us. What does stand out is that, despite being a peasant, Jesus could boast of a long-established lineage. Presumably his family would have clung to this small indicator of honor. What else would they have had, with a hometown like Nazareth? I do not know if you have ever visited Nazareth, but it is not a very impressive place. Halfway between the Sea of Galilee and the great Mediterranean Sea, it is dwarfed in size and quality of life by the great cities of Galilee that encircle it: Tiberias, a most impressive city built by Herod Antipas as his second Galilean capital; Sepphoris, rebuilt by Herod Antipas, itself the ornament of all Galilee; and the magnificent Hellenistic city-states of Scythopolis, Sidon, and Tyre, the last being one of the cities where I spent many years of my life. These are bustling cities on the international trade routes and are full of merchants and artisans selling the finer things of life to the elite inhabitants. By contrast, Nazareth has a mere five hundred inhabitants at most, predominately agricultural workers, and an inordinate number of peasant busybodies concerned only with one another's business. The town's main function is simply to supply the nearby city of Sepphoris with provisions. If the goal of your narrative is to demonstrate Jesus' claim to honor, it will have to cover a lot of ground.

In this regard, we were also struck by your description of the John who baptizes, the son of the priest Zechariah. He certainly seemed a troubled soul. His profile reminded me somewhat of a group of Jews who lived on the edge of the Dead Sea [a group now known as the Qumran community]. I think their community has now disbanded. I do not know much about them, except that, like John, they were very interested in baptism and lived in the wilderness. Moreover, they were not well regarded by some of the elite priests in Jerusalem with whom I occasionally came into contact. Perhaps those priests would not have appreciated John either. Am I right to think that there might have been some tension between Zechariah and John, the priestly father in the temple and the radical son in the wilderness? Both would have thought of themselves as agents of the Jewish god, but whereas the father offered sacrifices in the temple for the forgiveness of his people's sins, the son promoted "a baptism of repentance for the forgiveness of sins" [3:3]. Surely most Jews, and the priests in particular, considered the temple of their Jerusalem god to be the location where the forgiveness of sins took place prior to its destruction.

John also raised his voice against the lifestyle of Herod Antipas [3:19]. This caught my attention immediately since, despite the great numbers of Antipas' admirers, I consider myself to hold the greatest admiration for Herod Antipas. He had some Jewish heritage,[1] of course, whereas I do not. And yet, his name has been mine all my life, out of admiration

---

1. Antipas' father, Herod the Great, was an Idumean, and his mother, Malthace, was a Samaritan. Therefore, Antipas' Jewish heritage was weak, with Idumeans and Samaritans being looked upon by Jews as having compromised the bloodline of Jews.

for the way he advanced civic life in Galilee, much like his father, Herod the Great. My own father benefited much from Herod Antipas' Galilean initiatives, which promoted the ways of Rome and the economic advancement of the area. As a consequence, our family's material resources became firmly established. If Jesus the Nazarene is associated with John who baptizes and who opposed Herod Antipas, I will be intrigued to discover from your narrative whether Jesus followed the path of social unrest that John seems to flirt with or the path of honor. Jesus seems a curious figure in this regard.

These and other points were the focus of our recent discussion. We plan to meet again next week, and again I will write a digest of our discussion and send you sections of that digest by way of Stachys, unless you suggest otherwise. As ever, your care of Stachys is much appreciated. He speaks highly of you and of your hospitality. Please accept my gift of gratitude for your hospitality.

May the rains bring plenty to Calpurnius' fields, to the honor of the blessed emperor.

REPORT ON PERGAMENE GLADIATORIAL CONTESTS

Hosted by Gaius Rufinus, benefactor of Pergamum, in honor of his deceased father, Drusus, leading citizen of Pergamum, and in celebration of the bountiful goodness of the gods and the wisdom of their representative, our divine emperor Domitian.

The contests were held on the thirteenth day before the calends of April [19 March]. Festivities began the evening before the contests, when two banquets were sponsored. The first was held in the dining halls of the temple of Zeus for the benefit of noblemen and honored guests. The second was held in the halls of the upper gymnasium for the benefit of all the gladiatorial contestants. Vast amounts of food and drink were consumed in both feasts, although some of the contestants were unable to eat, overcome by fear at the prospect of what the next day might hold for them. A nearby temple was functioning to enable the contestants to offer sacrifices to Hercules, god of the gladiators. In the temple of Zeus, sacrifices were offered to the traditional gods of Rome and to the emperor.

On the day of the contests, the amphitheater was filled to capacity. Gaius Rufinus and the leading men of Pergamum were joined by representatives of twenty-one regional cities: Troas, Adramyttium, Thyratira, Sardis, Hypaepa, Philadelphia, Nysa, Hierapolis, Laodicea, Aphrodisias, Hyllarima, Halicarnassus, Iasus, Miletus, Priene, Ephesus, Colophon, Teos, Smyrna, Cyme, and Magnesia. The rest of the amphitheater contained residents from Pergamum and many from neighboring cities.

The day of the games began with a parade of the contestants. Accompanied by trumpet fanfares, they made an impressive display. Especially magnificent were the gladiators offered by the emperor himself for the occasion. Wearing fine purple cloaks with ornate gold embroidery, they paraded in chariots while their stewards carried their armory behind them.

them. The parade culminated in a spring dedication for a good harvest, with sacrifices offered to the goddess Flora on behalf of Domitian, our empire's father, lord, and god.

With the preliminaries complete, the morning beast hunt commenced. Spectators were delighted by the display of wild animals in the throws of life-and-death struggle: bears chained to bulls; wild cats and panthers chained to rhinoceroses; and lions chained to elephants. Later the *bestiarii* [humans trained to fight wild animals] and wild dogs entered the arena to combat with animals imported especially for slaughter: bears, elephants, tigers, deer, panthers, gazelles, rhinoceroses, lions, antelope, and bulls. The total number of beasts slaughtered was nearly three hundred; the total number of *bestiarii* slaughtered was only four.

Not long after the morning beast hunt ended, the gods kindly provided favorable weather for the rest of the day. Just after midday, the local boys who had removed the carcasses throughout the morning refreshed the bloodstained sand and spread new sand around the arena. Then the execution of criminals began, their number including murderers, arsonists, robbers, slave deserters, and those guilty of treason. Since Pergamum has "the right of sword" [the authority to carry out executions according to its own discretion, without approval from a higher authority], and since the city officials had granted "the right of sword" to these contests, the executions fell within the boundaries of imperial regulations. The execution of the freemen among the criminals proceeded along normal lines, as one by one they were thrust through with the blade of a sword. They combated in pairs, with one of the pair having been given a sword to overcome the other. His task completed, the sword was then passed to a new contestant, whose responsibility was to defeat the first. Fifteen freemen met their end in this way, with the sixteenth having his throat cut by a gladiator. Then the slaves among the criminal group met their fittingly dishonorable deaths. Twenty of them, many with their hands already amputated, were torn to bits one at a time by lions, bears, or panthers while chained to chariots or hanging from crosses. Eight were burned at the stake at strategic points around the amphitheater. One adulteress met her ignoble death strapped naked to the back of a bull.

Once the sand was again refreshed, the gladiatorial combat began early in the afternoon. The casting of lots had already taken place, determining the gladiatorial pairs. In order to provide the audience with added enjoyment, it was decided ahead of time that at least two gladiatorial contests should take place simultaneously. In just under four hours, 108 gladiators had competed, with 42 deaths. The lives of a few defeated gladiators were spared, since they fought bravely to the satisfaction of the masses and the host of the contests. In some contests both gladiators expired. Many met their deaths bravely. Most types of gladiators were represented, including the Thracians [using a shield, saber, and armor], the Samnites [using a shield, helmet, and short sword], the Retiarii [using a net and trident spear], and the Dimachaerii [using a dagger in each hand]. Of particular interest was the rare spectacle of the Catervarii [two-man gladiatorial teams fighting other two-man teams], of which there were eight teams. Also of interest were the ten women trained in gladiatorial combat who competed against one another, of which seven survived. The Pergamene precedent for this was established by the emperor Domitian, who sponsored a gladiatorial day in Pergamum two years ago [90 C.E.] in which there were contests among women and among dwarves or midgets.

Toward the end of the afternoon, Rufinus called a halt to the contests and awarded prizes of honor to the gladiators who provided the spectators with the most elaborate displays of strength, cunning, and bravery. Two gladiators in particular received highest honors: Diodorus and Castor, both owned by Photinus from Alexandria. Afterward, while the arena boys sold flasks of gladiators' blood to those in need of healing, a great banquet was provided for a large number of the spectators, in which copious reserves of wine and food were available, including olives, leeks, and specialty meats of boar, antelope, gazelle, and flamingo.

This day will long be remembered as one worthy of the most excellent Drusus, father of Rufinus, who has exceeded his peers in honoring our divine emperor and the gracious gods that beneficently oversee the glorious city of Pergamum, citadel of the gods and servant of the eternal city of Rome.

LUKE'S LETTER

Luke, servant of God;

To Antipas, servant of the people, and to Rufinus, nobleman of Pergamum;

Greetings.

The report of the Pergamene gladiatorial contests in honor of the noble Drusus makes clear that the spectators who had gathered for the event had no cause for disappointment, receiving what they had expected from the event. Rufinus, you should be pleased that your efforts to provide a grand spectacle were met with success. Informal accounts within Ephesus unanimously praise the event, suggesting that it will ensure the stature of Pergamum and the renowned host of the gladiatorial contests for some time to come. I will deposit the official report in the Ephesian archives.

Your letter, Antipas, caused me to rejoice when reading of your plans to send me a digest of your discussions of my monograph on Jesus. It would please me greatly to discuss the significance of the story with ones as diligent and attentive as you have shown yourselves to be. So I look forward to this dialogical enterprise and, if you so wish, commit myself to you as loyal friends in this partnership. You have witnessed many deaths recently, honorable noblemen of Pergamum; I recommend that you now consider the meaning of death in relation to the life of this simple Nazarene, who has changed the lives of many.

Let me respond, then, to the points you raised regarding John the baptizer. Here in Ephesus there is a community of Christians that includes within its constituency a significant number of people who previously followed the way of John the baptizer. Without regard for their personal fortune, they continue to speak the truth of God to whoever will listen. I have met with this group of Christians on several occasions, although the gathering of Christians with whom I am most closely associated here in Ephesus was originally founded by my friend and teacher, Paul of Tarsus, with whom I traveled extensively throughout the empire. But I have strayed from my point, which is simply that the baptizer's influence is still evident to this day, even in Ephesus, far separated from John by time and distance.

You are right to perceive some similarities between the baptizer and the somewhat idiosyncratic group of Jews based on the shores of the Dead Sea. The community of these devout separatist Jews is no longer in existence. But it did not disband. It was destroyed by the Roman troops during the Jewish uprising against Rome. This community on the shores of the Dead Sea resembled a larger group of Jews, the Essenes, a movement whose significance has greatly decreased since the destruction of the Jerusalem temple. Although there may still be some active members, I have no evidence of this.

From my previous travels throughout the region of Judea and from my reading of Josephus, I estimate that the Essenes had numbered about 4,000, with a notable presence in most of the towns of Judea and in one area of Jerusalem. One of Jerusalem's city gates was known as the Essene Gate. Although they berated the Jerusalem aristocracy and priesthood for their corruption and illegitimacy, the Essenes nonetheless continued to offer sacrifices at the Jerusalem temple. They were also critical of the way in which the Jerusalem temple was regulated by the priests according to a lunar calendar of 354 days per year, instead of their preferred solar calendar of 364 days, precisely 52 weeks. For the Essenes, the Jewish festivals as observed in Jerusalem were held on the incorrect days of the year and were out of alignment with the heavenly observances of those days.

The Essenes also instituted a closely prescribed system of initiation, with a three-year period of probation in order to prevent impurities from contaminating their membership. During the first year, one had to live according to the patterns of an Essene lifestyle but outside an Essene community. In the second and third years of probation, one could immerse oneself in the members' ritual baths but could not share in the common fellowship meals. Final admission into the movement involved taking serious oaths and the threat of complete expulsion if one did not strictly obey the elders and the corporate rules. Entrants turned all their property over to an Essene community. Each month, two days' wages were to be contributed simply for the purpose of supplying charity to their own members and to others in need. In the war against Rome, many of their members were active in the rebellion, with one of their number, known as John the Essene, being a renowned military governor of rebels in Thamna.

Most of these characteristics were shared by the community on the shores of the Dead Sea. Its members, however, formed a stricter faction within the larger Essene movement. The community would have consisted of two hundred people at the most at any given time. These members were instructed in the teachings of the community's founder, who was known as "the teacher of righteousness" and who had revealed to the community the true meaning of the holy writings, or so the community believed. The solar calendar of 364 days was strictly observed in this community, an act that put its members at odds with the Jerusalem high priesthood, which they considered to have become irremediably corrupt. These pious ones considered the temple sacrifices to be worthless and saw their own lifestyle of prayer and radical obedience to the law as a means of atonement for themselves and the land. The community members thought of themselves as the embodiment of God's pure people, since they alone had remained obedient to the God of Israel. Their community represented the true priesthood, and their community embodied the true temple. And so they waited in the wilderness, eagerly preparing for and expectant of the time when God would inaugurate his reign in association with his holy ones. They had long foreseen themselves involved at a future time in a great battle against Rome, fighting alongside the angelic hosts against the forces of darkness that included the forces of evil, the gentile nations, and the majority of Jews. The God of Israel was to take action to cleanse the corrupted land and temple. Under his oversight, the community would take control of the city of Jerusalem, implement the correct calendar, restore a legitimate priesthood, rebuild the temple according to its own architectural plans, and initiate patterns of lifestyle that were tightly controlled by purity regulations.

In some ways, Antipas, you are right to notice a degree of resemblance between John the baptizer and this devout community. John operated in the Judean wilderness, the same geographical terrain in which the Dead Sea community had chosen to operate (although John operated farther north). Both John and this community manifested ascetic tendencies. They both made much of water baptism. Both had priestly connections of some sort (although this might have been lost over time within the

Dead Sea community). They both believed that the priestly leadership of Israel was corrupt to the core. Both thought that forgiveness from God and right standing with him were possible apart from the temple apparatus in Jerusalem. They both found the same text from Isaiah to be a programmatic text: "In the desert prepare the way for the Lord; in the wilderness make straight a highway for our God" [Isa. 40:3]. Both believed that they lived in the time when the fulfillment of the promises of Israel's God would begin to transpire and that God's judgment on Israel was imminent, making repentance an urgent matter.

But these similarities can be overdone, since there were significant differences between them as well. Although some followed his lifestyle and teachings, John operated alone, as an isolated individual, apart from a community. He was intent on directly calling the nation to repentance, whereas the Dead Sea community preferred to withdraw from what its members saw as the polluted majority of Israel, having as little contact with others as possible and keeping its views hidden from outsiders. Unlike this community, John permitted the clean and the unclean, the sinners and the righteous, to come into contact with him. This may explain why even tax collectors and Roman soldiers approached John for instruction. You are probably correct to think that John's own father might have had difficulty accepting John's methods of dealing with sin and uncleanness. Whereas the Dead Sea community practiced baptismal washing to effect the purification of the body, John's rite of baptism was to effect the forgiveness of sins and bore resemblance to proselyte baptism, which was a ritual practiced only for the benefit of the unclean gentiles. In John's view, the Jewish nation needed more than remedial attention to minor problems; it needed to start afresh before God. All people were invited to the radical challenge, regardless of whether they were seen as clean or unclean, righteous or sinner. In this way, John the baptizer is much like the Jesus whose story you have before you. Both were men of honor, I believe, who lived and died committed to the ways of the good and the right.

I have kept Stachys a day longer than usual in order to respond properly to your insightful points regarding John and his relationship to this group and to Jesus. While I researched and dictated my response, Stachys made himself a benefit to Calpurnius' household.

I very much enjoy hearing how you are reading my monograph and will look forward to receiving a digest of material in due course. I will endeavor to respond appropriately to your digests. I also trust that the

Spirit of God will enlighten you as to the significance of Jesus' life. In my experience, one cannot become familiar with the story of Jesus without also being challenged by it. In fact, let me suggest to you, friends and partners in discussion, that you track down some of the followers of Jesus who live in Pergamum and ask to attend their gatherings. Some Christians gather in the house of Antonius, as you already know. Their corporate life will itself testify to the veracity of my monograph. Another group of Christians also meets in Pergamum, although I know very little about their gathering except that it meets in the house of Kalandion, a prominent citizen, who must be the same Kalandion who assisted in the organization of the recent Pergamene gladiatorial contests. No doubt he would welcome your presence in their gathering.

May God bless you.[2]

---

2. Speculative dates for this correspondence might be as follows: Stachys departs from Pergamum on the morning of 25 March, arriving in Ephesus on the afternoon of 28 March, staying for one additional day; Stachys leaves Ephesus for Pergamum on the morning of 30 March, carrying Luke's reply and arriving in Pergamum on 3 April.

JESUS'
NAIVE AND
IRRESPONSIBLE
VIEWS

[The following letter from Antipas introduces two of his "conversational digests" written on two separate occasions after discussing Luke's text with Rufinus. I have identified them as digest 1 and digest 2. Luke's response to digest 1 was written later but is included here to suit the dialogical character of this correspondence. No response to digest 2 has been discovered.]

Antipas' Letter

Antipas, esteemed citizen and dialogue partner with Luke of Ephesus;

To Luke, trustworthy historian and friend;

Greetings.

With the arrival of spring, the rich cultural offerings of Pergamum are more evident than ever, and I am enjoying the beauty of the region. It is good for me to get out and enjoy the surrounding countryside. I have to admit to having a touch of arthritis in my joints, and the movement of exercise is proving beneficial to me. I had hoped that the god Asklepios would look kindly upon me if I relocated here in Pergamum. Prior to my departure from Caesarea, I had heard reports about a tremendous resurgence in miracles performed at the Pergamene Asklepion. Pilgrims seeking healing continue to flood into the city at a steady pace. Some of them report spectacular miracles. For my part, I can only testify that Asklepios has been helped by the sun, whose rays have recently been strong and therapeutic.

Attached to this letter you will find two brief digests of my recent discussions with Rufinus concerning your monograph. We continue to be impressed with your compositional style and enamored with your narrative.

The gift that Stachys carries is given sincerely.

May mighty Jupiter, together with your own god, continue to look favorably upon you.

LUKE'S LETTER

Luke, lover of God;

To Antipas and Rufinus, noblemen and civic benefactors;

Greetings.

Stachys has arrived to a busy household. We are preparing a feast and expect many local Christians to join us in rejoicing before God. So I must be brief. To add to our joy, we have received news that Calpurnius arrived safely in Caesarea after a six-day journey by ship. He is probably in Jerusalem even as I write this.

Clearly, your engagement with my monograph on Jesus honors me greatly. I am in your debt. Nonetheless, having read quickly through your two digests, I feel constrained to write with urgent advice. It is imperative that you seek out the Christians who gather in the house of Antonius. Your experiences in the house of Kalandion [see digest 2 below] are not representative of all Christian gatherings. A full investigation of the matter requires your attendance at the gathering of Christians in Antonius' house. They would be eager to meet with you, and you could send them my greetings. They regularly discuss what they know of Jesus and would welcome the chance to hear my monograph about him. In fact, some from among their number are seeking to live their lives on the basis of Jesus' own lifestyle, so you could inquire of them about your concerns. A few among their number, such as Antonius and his wife, Mania, are wellborn, so you would have peers among their gathering.

I will respond to your digests as time permits. I expect to be able to send my responses with Stachys when he next visits us.

Stachys has endeared himself with Calpurnius' household. He is welcome here always, even when most of Calpurnius' household is engrossed in celebratory preparation.

May the father of our Lord Jesus Christ be gracious to you.

ANTIPAS' DIGEST 1

[The text discussed is Luke 5–6.]

I met with Rufinus earlier this week to read and discuss more of your narrative about the Jew Jesus. Despite your assurances that he was not a disrupter of society, we nonetheless found him to be a disturbing figure.

First, he made utopian promises to the peasants, promising them a share in the empire of the Jewish god, in which they will have plenty. The poor frequently have utopian dreams, and perhaps they should, since those dreams help to make the hardships of peasant life more bearable. Jesus seems to have given the peasants what they needed to hear. Evidently, even revolutionaries plotting the overthrow of Rome were attracted to this message to the poor, since Jesus had within his number a man named Simon whom you say "was called the Zealot" [6:15]—which I assume refers not simply to a character trait of zeal but to a passionate interest in replacing Roman rule with Jewish independence.[1] Of course, any utopian hopes conjured up by Jesus can no longer be sustained in the name of the Jewish god. That god is clearly impotent against the power of the gods of Rome, having been utterly trounced by them in the demolition of the city of Jerusalem, where he was said to dwell.

Second, Jesus blatantly castigated the rich elite. To us, he sounds like just another of the uninformed peasantry who frequently murmur behind our backs, grumbling against us but all the time failing to see that we are not at fault for their condition. We provide those in our households with the necessities they require and with security against the ravages of life.

---

1. Antipas understands the term "Zealot" to designate the resistance movement of "Zealots" that emerged just before the Jewish revolt of 66–70 C.E. It is unlikely, however, that the Zealots had emerged as a coordinated movement during the time of Jesus. This makes Antipas' identification of Simon as a "Zealot" somewhat problematic. Nonetheless, the same Simon is remembered in other Gospels as "the Cananaean" (Matt. 10:4; Mark 3:18), a term having revolutionary connotations. So Antipas' interpretation may not be far from the mark. Originally, the epithet "zealot" probably indicated Simon's zeal for the law, a zeal that included an anti-Roman stance most clearly embodied in the later Zealot movement.

Those beyond our households benefit from our benefaction to the cities: the paved streets, the public baths, the amphitheaters, the attractions of the civilized world. And in times of famine, it is frequently our warehouses of grain that feed the masses. Why are we deserving of Jesus' condemnation in the name of his god? Our gods have obviously favored us and been gracious to us, and we in turn are gracious to others. In a sense, then, those of us who are rich exemplify some of the very attributes that Jesus himself espoused, doing good to those who hate us and being merciful to those in need.

Third, Jesus upheld an impractical standard of living. He simply did not understand how this world works. To lend without expecting repayment [6:35] would only undermine the reputation of efficient householders, leaving them vulnerable to direct violations from competitors and ultimately leading to financial ruin. I would not advise my son to operate the family business in this way. If he loaned money without expecting repayment of the loan and its interest, our financial enterprises would simply collapse. How would that be of benefit to those who are supported by my son's household? Except for the few fortunate men who might be able to find employment in the household of another rich man, most of them would have to become day laborers or beggars, and many women would be forced into prostitution. Most of these options are dead ends. If all Jesus had to offer was the collapse of the household structures that prop up all that is good within our society, was he not simply a social miscreant and a menace? I am starting to think that perhaps he was another antisocial fanatic, like his cousin, John the baptizer, the denouncer of Herod Antipas.

But one thing puzzled us. You describe Jesus as having among his followers not only Simon the Zealot but also Levi, who collected duty from travelers for Rome's benefit. What an unlikely combination! The one was prepared to murder others in order to weaken Rome's grip of peace, while the other helped to oil the machinery of Roman administration. This is remarkable. I know of no precedent for bringing together in partnership people whose interests are so diametrically opposed. Zealots have been known to murder Jewish tax collectors, who are usually despised as collaborators in the Roman system. The uniting of two such opposed figures can only be explained, I suspect, by their common interest in Jesus' miraculous powers, making them willing to forgo their differences to have a stake in that power.

By the way, I know something of the Pharisees, but I found myself rather poor at explaining for Rufinus' benefit their interests and history. My interests in Galilee were purely financial, and my efforts in Caesarea and Tyre were largely given to promoting the magnificent advances of Rome. I never had much need to cultivate an interest in the intricacies of Jewish religion. If you find time to send us a brief profile of the Pharisees, it would enhance Rufinus' appreciation of your perplexing narrative.

Luke's Response to Digest 1

In many ways, good Antipas and noble Rufinus, I am in agreement with your assessment of the main character of my narrative. Jesus did, in fact, hold out the promise of better things to the poor among whom he lived, not only in the age to come but already in the present, as God's empire begins to take hold. And with regard to the way that the elite such as yourselves bring benefits to many, there can be no doubt. In fact, in volume two of my monograph, I demonstrate the extent to which the spread of Christianity has itself benefited from the generosity of elite benefactors.

But benefaction is only one means of civic beneficence, and it may have its own weaknesses and deficiencies. In my travels and studies, I have met many who simply fell through the rather large gaps in the safety nets of benefaction. The poor and diseased already permeate the countryside and infiltrate cities throughout the empire. Their very presence is a testimony to the fact that Rome's power does not extend to eradicating this imbalance in the social register. From my understanding, Jesus recognized that benefaction can promote the good for some factions of society, but he nonetheless advocated a different model of promoting the good in what he envisaged as the empire of the God of Israel.

With regard to Jesus' impractical and unrealistic expectations, I am in full agreement. In my opinion, the human heart that empowers society does not seem able to live up to the standards that Jesus set in his style of life and death. But that, my friend, is to get ahead of you in the narrative. Calpurnius always chides me for saying little about what I believe and writing much about it. I think this is his way of teasing me for having written such a lengthy monograph. He himself is not a lover of books like his father, Theophilus. But since he is probably correct about my tendency to dictate with verbosity, I will refrain from writing more in response to your intriguing views of Jesus as depicted in my narrative. To learn more of my own views, you need only to read further.

My next task is to respond to your request for assistance by giving a fuller portrait of the Pharisees than that which emerges in my monograph. From what I can gather, the Pharisees began to emerge as a distinct group within Judaism about 150 years before the birth of Jesus. They were one of the Jewish factions that stood against the imposition of Greek ideals and practices upon Jews. Their corporate name "Pharisees" seems to derive from the Hebrew word meaning "separate"; they are "separate ones" in regard to their distinctive and stringent observance of the Jewish law. The Pharisees have had some success in influencing political rulers over the Jewish people, but for the most part they have remained a peripheral party in the political processes of Judea and Galilee. Toward the end of the reign of Herod the Great (that is, around the time of Jesus' birth), the Pharisees numbered approximately six thousand, indicating something of their significance in certain sectors of Palestinian society.

In the time of Jesus, their prime interest was in controlling the laws that governed Jewish life, and their real agenda was the hallowing of everyday life in all its aspects while living within the existing structures of society. They are noted for their meticulous attention to the practice of the law of Moses. In particular, they focus their attention on dietary laws, ritual purity for meals, and the observance of the sabbath.

They also claim to be the faithful transmitters of the oral traditions originally given to Moses on Mount Sinai. Like the Dead Sea community, they too claim to have the correct interpretation of the Jewish law. They explain and expand the law to meet new dilemmas and situations, thinking it better to be prepared for a situation in advance than to be unprepared; the danger of encountering an unforeseen situation is that one might devise rules to suit one's personal preferences. They believe in bodily resurrection after death, unlike the Sadducees, who tend to be of higher social station than the Pharisees and are not interested in an afterlife.

Jesus was a contemporary of two of the greatest Pharisees in recent memory, Hillel and Shammai. Generally speaking, Hillel held a somewhat lenient view of things, and Shammai usually adopted a much more stringent view of matters. Each had a group of Pharisaic adherents, and the debates between these two Pharisaic groups are legendary even to this day. By the way, I have heard an amusing story, probably apocryphal, regarding these two legendary figures. It is said that a gentile approached

Rabbi Shammai, saying, "Rabbi, if you can teach me the whole of the law and the prophets while I stand on one foot, I will convert." Shammai had no time for the man and sent him away. The man then went to Rabbi Hillel with the same prospect. Hillel's response was simply this: "What is hateful to you, do not do to your neighbor. That is the whole Torah. The rest is commentary thereon; go and learn it."

Ringing in my ears now are Calpurnius' words about my verbosity whenever I dictate to my scribe. Perhaps this brief portrait may be of some assistance to you and especially Rufinus as you read further.

Antipas' Digest 2

[The text discussed is Luke 7–8.]

Rufinus and I did as you suggested [see Luke's letter in the sixth letter collection] by attending a gathering of Jesus worshipers. It was convenient to meet with those in the house of Kalandion, since he and Rufinus have a relationship of friendship that goes back a long way. Rufinus contacted Kalandion earlier in the week about the prospect of our attendance at the gathering, and Kalandion was quick to extend an invitation for us to join the gathering in his magnificent house (located where the High Street meets the Lower Agora). So on the "Lord's Day" (as they call it) we were warmly welcomed into their midst. Along with Kalandion's household there were sixteen who gathered, mostly wealthy artisans and merchants. Lycomedes, along with several members of his household, was also in attendance for the first time. He is among the most influential citizens of Pergamum, like Kalandion himself. (It may interest you to know that Lycomedes is the uncle of Earinus, the emperor's "favorite boy,"[2] who was raised here in Pergamum. Evidently, it was Lycomedes who persuaded Earinus to use his influence with the emperor in order to benefit the city, and consequently Domitian himself has recently made a sizable donation to the Pergamene cult of Asklepios.)

Rufinus had already mentioned to Kalandion that I have in my possession a copy of your monograph about Jesus, and Kalandion encouraged me to bring it with me to the gathering. I was pleased to do so, and the gatherers were eager to hear something read from it. Rather than starting from the beginning, I simply carried on from the point at which Rufinus and I had stopped last week. After eating with Lycomedes, Rufinus, and myself in the triclinium [the dining room reserved for special guests],

---

2. A sexual relationship is intimated here.

Kalandion gathered the whole group together in the atrium [the large main courtyard of the house]. There I read aloud, trying to bring out the intrigue of your narrative with my voice, as if in a performance. Everyone enjoyed the reading, and we discussed it for some time afterward.

For my part, I was again interested in comparing John who baptizes and Jesus. You seem to portray the two as similar in some respects and different in others. You depict Jesus as forgiving the sins of a sinful woman [7:48]. In that regard, he can be likened to John since, for both, divine forgiveness is not restricted to the Jerusalem temple.

But you also portray them as having different attitudes concerning lifestyle. John strikes a strongly ascetic profile in his own lifestyle, "neither eating bread nor drinking wine" and, as Rufinus and I read last week, gathering to himself disciples who "often fast and pray." Despite having been baptized by John, however, Jesus chose a different lifestyle, one of "eating and drinking" and being a friend of tax collectors and sinners. (On this score, I have known many like Jesus in my time!) He chose Levi, the one who collected taxes for Rome, as one of his closest associates, and you suggest that other tax collectors were also favorably impressed with him. Your narrative even suggests that a Roman centurion was attracted to Jesus for the supernatural power that he commanded [7:1–10]. I was especially interested to see Joanna, the wife of Chuza, who used to manage the finances of Herod Antipas' own household, appearing in your narrative as a supporter of Jesus [8:3]. Whereas John who baptizes was beheaded by Antipas, Jesus was assisted by one in Antipas' household. The contrast is glaring. I had expected to find that only the destitute and the peasantry would find attraction in Jesus' message, but clearly your narrative suggests that Jesus had a broader appeal than that. For that reason I consider Jesus to be a more attractive figure than John. Having been worried that Jesus was an antisocial disrupter, I now am hopeful that his interests in promoting a healthy society may not have been much different from my own.

I pointed all this out to those who gathered at Kalandion's house, and they all agreed. But I had some trouble with the way they interpreted who Jesus was. They were mostly interested in the stories of Jesus' power, as displayed in the healings, exorcisms, and the sea miracle that you narrate. Obviously, this is a significant part of his profile, but other aspects of his identity failed to be of import for those in Kalandion's house. I mentioned, for instance, the agitation Rufinus and I had felt earlier concerning Jesus'

somewhat naive and irresponsible views about wealth and material possessions, as in my previous digest. I suggested that we discuss what Jesus
meant by "the poor have good news preached to them" [7:22], pointing
out that earlier Jesus had staked his reputation on working for the benefit of the oppressed [4:16–21], but no one seemed interested in that topic.

In my view, this is a crucial matter that your narrative has thus far
posed, but the point was met with somewhat lukewarm interest from
those in Kalandion's house. Whereas Jesus' teachings of peasant wisdom
had stirred up animosity in me, for the most part those same teachings
met with apathy among most of those who gathered with Kalandion.
They seem almost exclusively interested in stories of Jesus' miraculous
power that reveal him to be one through whom the power of the gods
operated in an unprecedented manner. Many in Kalandion's house seem
to think that Neptune of the sea looked favorably on Jesus when he calmed
the storm [8:22–25], or that the healing power of Asklepios was active in
the healing of the centurion's servant, the widow's son, the demon-pos-
sessed man, the dead girl, and the sick woman [7:1–10, 11–17; 8:26–39,
40–56]. A Jesus of such power, who acts as a conduit for divine power of
various kinds, is good to have as a suprahuman benefactor, overseeing
one's household and blessing it with good things. I would agree with this,
of course, were it not for the fact that such a view seems to leave out so
much of the profile of Jesus of Nazareth, at least as you have depicted
him. Moreover, the cures normally associated with Asklepios bear little
resemblance to those of Jesus. Asklepios' cures are notably affected by
dream therapy, with additional dietary regulations for extended periods.
In their sleep, patients at the temple of Asklepios are said to meet a god
whose attendant applies medicines and potions, while a sacred serpent or
a temple dog licks the afflicted part of their bodies. The Asklepion priests
then interpret the dream and prescribe a diet of white pepper and onions,
with very little liquids. These are not the healing techniques of Jesus. So
I continue to be puzzled, both by the main figure in your narrative and
by the way those gathered at Kalandion's house interpret him.

Incidentally, good Luke, you may have heard the amusing report about
a recent healing in the Asklepion of Corinth. Evidently, a local woman
was met in her dream by Asklepios. Wanting to conceive a child with her
husband, she requested that the baby be a girl. Asklepios agreed to this
request, asking whether she desired anything else, but she did not. The
woman became pregnant, but after three years of pregnancy she still had

not given birth. Returning to the Asklepion, she again met Asklepios in a dream and asked why he had failed to keep his promise to her. Asklepios replied that he had kept his promise to enable her to conceive a girl; he had made no promise about the birth of the girl, since the woman had originally wanted nothing further from him. Nonetheless, since she returned to make supplication, Asklepios committed himself to permit the birth. Upon waking, the woman left the temple and gave birth to the three-year-old girl on the steps of the temple. Of course this must be a legend. If the gods treated us all with such anarchic cleverness, we would be subject to overwhelming chaos.[3]

3. If the previous letter to Luke was written on 24 March, and if Antipas was working on a weekly schedule, then the writing of digest 1 should be placed around 2 April and of digest 2 around 9 April. The cover letter was probably composed on 9 April and sent via Stachys on the morning of 10 April. Stachys arrived in Ephesus on the afternoon of 13 April and left on the morning of 14 April, returning to Pergamum on 17 April. He returned with Luke's brief letter (above). Luke's response to digest 1 was written at a later date, sometime between 14 April and 23 April.

LETTER
COLLECTION 8

COMMUNITIES
OF SUPPORT
AND FELLOWSHIP

Antipas' Letter

[The text discussed is Luke 9–10.]

Antipas, benefactor and servant of the people;

To Luke, friend and scholar;

Greetings.

For once, dear Luke, some of the information you sent to me proved to be antiquated, but only with regard to one bit of advice: your advice to seek out those Christians gathering at the house of Antonius and his splendid wife, Mania [see Luke's letter in letter collection 7]. By the time I received your letter, I had already attended a gathering of Christians at their house. Antonius himself sought me out and invited me. He had heard that I had attended the gathering at the house of Kalandion and also that I have a copy of your monograph. He suggested that I join them on the following Lord's Day and bring the manuscript along with me. Since I had made no commitment to those in the house of Kalandion, I was free to do as he suggested. (Rufinus, on the other hand, felt a debt of honor to Kalandion and preferred to meet once again with those at Kalandion's house.)

After an ample meal, Antonius suggested that I read an extract from your manuscript, which I was happy to do. The reading was then discussed among the gathering, although only a handful of us were active in the discussion, the others preferring simply to listen to our exchanges. There then followed a period of singing and prayer, although I quietly excused myself from that part of the evening and returned to Euphemos' house, since it was clear that these Christians cherish their singular devotion to Jesus in a way that made me somewhat uncomfortable.

89

Let me tell you, Luke my friend, that this group of twenty-five or so people meeting in Antonius' house is very different from that which gathers in the house of Kalandion. One thing struck me from the moment of being welcomed among them: The gatherers are very diverse with regard to their social statures, ethnic backgrounds, and civic positions. A similar kind of diversity of membership is sometimes evident in civic or trade associations, but not often to the same extent as I found in Antonius' house. Moreover, at no point did those gathered seem particularly interested in regulating their behavior according to social codes. This was especially evident when the food was brought out from the kitchens. At that point, the gatherers simply assembled themselves in small groups throughout the house, without any special interest in arranging themselves according to social customs of honor. I have never seen members of associations act in that fashion.

Among those gathered in Antonius' house, there were many poor artisans and urban day laborers. A few gatherers hold civic positions in the city and have sizable resources. Antonius himself is one of these, of course, currently holding the position of City Custodian of the Royal Treasuries of Pergamene Art, a collection kept in the Sanctuary of Athena, the oldest sanctuary in Pergamum. (Previously, he acted as the Protector of the city's Fountain House and oversaw the thermal baths that lie along a stretch of Pergamum's main road.) Mania herself is a capable municipal archontess [an elected official], formerly a priestess in the Sanctuary of Demeter, a cult dedicated to honoring all the known and unknown deities and extolling the virtues of civic and familial harmony. Some of those gathered have been Pergamenes from birth, such as Antonius and Mania, while others (mostly artisans) have moved here from other parts of Asia Minor, as well as from Italy, Macedonia, and Greece. A few Jews were also present. Some of them maintain a strict Jewish diet of kosher food, and for them special dietary provisions were made. I think one or two brought their own food.

One Jew deserves special mention—a Simon ben Joseph who hails from Galilee. I was introduced to him during the meal and was surprised to discover a most coincidental fact. This Simon used to be a tenant farmer who worked part of my own land northwest of Tiberias in Galilee. Having tested him on some details regarding my land tracts and household, I am convinced of the veracity of this fact. He is no longer in employment with my household because his lease agreement was canceled by my commercial manager several years ago; evidently, as a result of a serious crop failure one harvest season, Simon was unable to meet his required quota of production, and his tenancy was revoked. Simon explained that his subsequent efforts to work as a day laborer were not successful, and I can see why. His best years lie behind him, and he would no doubt be passed over in a manager's search for effective manual laborers. He recounted how my manager did provide him with work sporadically after his tenancy was rescinded, but evidently this situation did not last long. My manager began to conscript younger men for occasional work not long after having annulled Simon's contract as a tenant farmer, and Simon was rarely conscripted by other managers.

Never before have I encountered a former employee, so I found myself in an uncomfortable situation. The unfortunate man was forced to leave the members of his family to fend for themselves in Galilee. He fears that his daughters are now prostitutes or slaves and that his sons have scattered, perhaps to become beggars in the cities or bandits in the hills. He moved to Pergamum not to abandon them but to try to secure employment with the high hope of sending them some meager contributions to their well-being. He had heard of the significant expansion that Pergamum has recently been undergoing and hoped that he could find regular work in some form of construction.

The Pergamene trade guilds are powerful, however, and make it extremely difficult for ordinary unskilled day laborers to be conscripted for work of any kind. This is especially true of the stonemasons' guild, which has civic influence far beyond that of comparable guilds in other cities of the empire. So I was not surprised to discover that, contrary to his hopes, Simon was unable to find regular employment in Pergamum. He soon became a street beggar, and his condition worsened until he gave up all hope of living. He told me, however, that as he squatted hopeless, diseased, and destitute on the Pergamene streets, he was noticed by Antonius himself, who extended hospitality to him, bringing him into his own house and ensuring that he was restored to health. Simon has served in Antonius' household for just over a year, ever since his recovery. Although he maintains a level of Jewish purity, Antonius and Mania have provided for his needs in that regard as well. To look at him now, you would never know of the harshness of his former condition, except for a certain shortness of breath that overcomes him at times. His spirits are high, and he has a laugh that is robust and infectious. He plans to return to Galilee soon, in the hopes of tracking down whatever remains of his family and bringing them to Pergamum with him, with Antonius' blessing and assistance.

I must confess to having a sense of admiration for this Simon, which is strange because he is so obviously below my own station. Perhaps, since we both spent most of our lives in the eastern Mediterranean, I am simply confusing a sense of shared experiences with a sense of goodwill. But this is not really a satisfactory explanation, since our experiences of Galilee cannot be considered "shared," being so vastly different. Despite his low status, there seems to be a kind of nobility in him—a nobility that I would not expect to see in the eyes of one upon whom the gods have not looked favorably. Perhaps Antonius has instilled this sense of nobility within him. But then I am forced to consider Antonius' own actions in this matter. What nobleman stoops down in the street to pick up a diseased beggar and care for him? Such an action is completely impractical by any standard of common sense. Imagine the danger to Antonius and his household if Simon had been a practitioner of the evil eye. Although it became clear that he was not a manipulator of pernicious spirits, Antonius had no way of knowing that at the time. Moreover, Antonius must certainly have compromised his public honor in the flagrant act of extending hospitality to an expendable such as Simon had been. All of my natural impulses are repelled by the thought of Antonius' action, and my instincts label it an impractical, irresponsible, and ultimately dishonorable action. And yet there was Simon, standing before me in Antonius' house, with honor in his eyes—a testament to Antonius' unprecedented benevolence.

With regard to your narrative of Jesus' life, my experiences with those who gathered at Antonius' house impressed upon me how capable they were of interpreting your monograph after I had read them a portion of it. Whereas those who gathered at Kalandion's house seemed to be interested only in the stories of Jesus' miraculous power, those gathered in Antonius' house focused not on the miraculous exclusively but also on the radical lifestyle Jesus endorsed. They seem to know what Jesus meant by taking up one's despised cross daily, and they approved of the implication that the foolish person seeks worldly gain while losing one's very self [9:23–27]. They understood and affirmed Jesus' inversion of the definition of "greatness" [9:46–48]. I was especially impressed by their interest in Jesus' story of the Samaritan who acted like a neighbor to one who lay half dead by the roadside [10:30–37]. Simon mentioned his own resemblance to the half-dead man in that parable and Antonius' resemblance to the Samaritan, but the gatherers' primary interest was not to laud members for past actions but to reinforce a concern to help others in the future. In particular, they used the occasion of reflecting on this parable as a time to take an inventory of the gatherers' needs for the forthcoming week and to arrange for many of those needs to be met, largely through Antonius' resources, but not exclusively so. Evidently, foodstuffs were provided earlier in the week for some of the artisans and their colleagues, even some who were not normal gatherers at Antonius' house. Something similar is planned for others in the forthcoming week.

My friend, I have spoken at length about my encounter with this group of Christians, and I apologize if I have gone on too long. I have taken a curious interest in them. Many of them know of you, of course, since you have visited them on previous occasions when traveling through Pergamum. Those who know you speak highly of you and requested that I send you their greetings. Antonius and Mania look forward to your next visit.

By the way, upon delivering this letter, Stachys will also deliver to you a short overview of the Samaritans, which I myself have composed. While discussing your text at Antonius' house, several gatherers queried whether there was significance in the fact that the man who acted as a neighbor was a Samaritan as opposed to a Jew. Along with one or two others, I was able to contribute something to the discussion about the Samaritans, but it was Simon especially who was able to assist the rest of us in understanding some of the particulars of their history and identity. I drafted this small overview the following day, which I am sending to you out of respect for your own interests and abilities as a competent historian. No doubt much of this is already known by you. In any event, feel free to dispose of it as you wish.

Stachys speaks highly of you and those in the household of Calpurnius. The gift he offers you is sent with gratitude.

May you continue to prosper, and may the household of Calpurnius increase in honor.

ANTIPAS' HISTORICAL RECONSTRUCTION: THE SAMARITANS

According to ancient Jewish traditions, the origins of Samaritan identity are traceable to the time of the Assyrian invasion of the land of Israel [722–721 B.C.E.], when some of the Israelites were taken into Assyrian exile. These traditions identify Samaritans as half-breeds, due to intermarriage with the Assyrians. Upon the return of many Jews from exile, a rivalry and antipathy developed between the Jews who had kept their bloodline pure and those who had intermingled their bloodline with that of the Assyrians (i.e., the Samaritans). Differences in practices mark the two groups, especially with regard to the location of the temple in which to offer sacrifices. For the Samaritans, the holy mountain for the temple site is Gerizim in Samaria, while for the Jews it is Zion in Judea. The Samaritans have a smaller canon of scripture than the Jews, accepting only the five books of the lawgiver Moses as their sacred scriptures. They share the expectations of many of the Jews that a special figure will arrive who will restore their fortunes. According to the Samaritans, this one will be a prophet like Moses who will reestablish true worship on Mount Gerizim. At one point, the Samaritans built their own temple on Mount Gerizim [ca. 388 B.C.E.], but it was destroyed roughly 150 years later by the Jewish Hasmonean ruler John Hyrcanus [128 B.C.E.]. This act further intensified the animus between the Samaritans and the Jews, feelings that later developed into outright racial hatred, continuing to this day.

Luke's Letter

Luke, servant of God;

To Antipas, servant of the people;

Greetings.

I am pleased that you met the Christians who gather at the house of Antonius and Mania. They are my brothers and sisters in the Lord, and I cherish their affections.

I am most appreciative of your efforts to outline something of Samaritan history. I found your outline to be helpful and have asked for it to be included in Theophilus' library in Calpurnius' house. If you continue to read my two volumes, you will find other interesting episodes in which Samaritans feature.

There is, however, one feature of your outline that I think needs qualification, and that is your last comment: "outright racial hatred, continuing to this day." Granted, hatred is frequently exhibited in relationships between most Jews and Samaritans, but this is not always the case. Here in Ephesus, for instance, a group of Christians consists of a significant Samaritan contingency, along with others who are Jews, as well as gentiles. They eat together and worship God together without racial animosity of the kind you mention because they have found their common life as followers of Jesus to be more important than their ethnic differences. (This is the group I mentioned to you on an earlier occasion that includes a significant number of former followers of John the baptizer who now worship Jesus as God's son.) You will find similar configurations of ethnic diversity among many gatherings of Christians throughout the world, some of which are known to me personally from my travels. They include communities in Rome, Corinth, Beroea, Thessalonica,

Philippi, Troas, Smyrna, Philadelphia, Pisidian Antioch, Iconium, Lystra, Derbe, and Syrian Antioch. I believe you have already seen something of this diversity even within the gathering of those who meet at Antonius' house. For many years mutuality between Jews and gentiles at common meals proved to be a controversial matter for Christians. Most Christian gatherings, however, have now found ways of accommodating that mutuality, since it is seen as an important sign of how the God that we worship is creating new communities of support and fellowship in ways that transcend usual ethnic boundaries without eradicating ethnic differences.

You might be interested to know that the group of Ephesian Christians to which I have already referred organizes itself around the leadership of a man named John, a Jew by birth who himself was an eyewitness to many of the events of Jesus' life. The community has had its difficulties in recent years, and some who hold to unhelpful beliefs have left to form their own community elsewhere. Unfortunately, John himself has recently died, but before his death he too assembled a manuscript about Jesus' life. I have read sections of his account with great profit. It differs from mine in several ways, since we draw out different aspects of Jesus' life. Nonetheless, our accounts are in complete agreement on the main features of Jesus' significance. Consequently, I have been asked by some of John's closest associates to work with them in editing and preparing John's manuscript for wider circulation, something we hope to do in the near future.

There is an expression I have picked up somewhere in my travels: "The bigger the empire, the smaller the world." Perhaps your encounter with Simon, your former tenant farmer, reflects that saying to some extent. I have met Simon on an earlier visit and on that occasion learned something of his history, although I never learned the specifics of his employment to the extent that you have recounted them. (In particular, he never mentioned the name of the landowner for whom he worked.) Antonius' own kindness toward Simon is certainly exceptional in the empire, not least since the social, economic, and ethnic profiles of the two men are dramatically different. But I would beg to differ with you regarding Antonius' "unprecedented" act of kindness, as you call it. Similar acts are displayed in Christian communities throughout the empire. Granted, not many Christians are in a position to do as much for a person in need as Antonius is, with his vast resources. But Antonius' actions are themselves merely reflections of the beneficence of the one we worship, Jesus Christ.

His life story modeled beneficence toward others, and he called his followers to pattern their lives on his own. Both John and I agree wholeheartedly on these points, as do most Christians. Antonius' act of benevolence is outweighed by the extent and significance of Jesus' benevolence, because it was Jesus' act of kindness that reveals, we believe, the very heart of the sovereign God and judge of this world.

Your own kindness, Antipas, is greatly appreciated, evident in the manner that you continue to help me understand how my monograph is being read and interpreted. I remain in your debt and look forward to your next letter. I have again insisted that Stachys remain in Calpurnius' household an extra night before returning to you so that I might write a proper reply to your letter.

May the God of goodness prepare your way.[1]

---

1. Assuming that Antipas is writing on the same weekly schedule, he would have written his letter on 16 April, the day before Stachys returned from Ephesus. Stachys probably left Pergamum for Ephesus on the morning of 18 April, arriving in Ephesus on the afternoon of 21 April. Staying at Calpurnius' household an extra day (as Luke mentions), he would then have left Ephesus on the morning of 23 April, carrying with him Luke's letter and arriving in Pergamum on 26 April.

THE CONTEXTS
DETERMINED
THE CONTENTS

[The following letter introduces the three additional "conversational digests" that Antipas wrote on three separate occasions after discussing Luke's text with others. I have identified Antipas' digests as digest 3, digest 4, and digest 5. Luke's responses to digests 3 and 4 are recorded here. A reply to digest 5 has not been discovered.]

Antipas' Letter

Antipas, seeker of truth and benefactor of the people;

To Luke, friend and scholar;

Greetings.

Stachys carries with my gift and this brief letter three digests of my conversations with others regarding your monograph. As you can see, there was a noticeable variety in the contexts in which my conversations were held, and I suspect that the contexts themselves determined the content of our discussions.

Thank you for your comments on the Samaritans. I was interested to hear that Samaritans are frequently accepted within Christian associations throughout the Mediterranean basin.

Those Christians known to you who meet in the house of Antonius send you their greetings.

I pray for your continued health and for that of Calpurnius.

LUKE'S LETTER

Luke, servant of God;

To Antipas, benefactor and esteemed nobleman;

Greetings.

    I am much in your debt upon receiving your three informative digests. I am eager to respond to your queries and will in due course send you my own views about the term "Son of Man" and the man Pontius Pilate [Luke's writings on these topics appear below].

    In response to your last digest, I have only to say that, in my experience, the combination of the story of Jesus, a community of love, and the moving of God's Spirit frequently results in new and surprising patterns of life, as you yourself have perhaps unwittingly experienced. I, along with the Christians who meet in the house of Calpurnius, will continue to pray on your behalf to the most high God, whose grace exceeds all bounds.

    This letter is sent with Stachys, your servant and a welcome sojourner. May God bless you.

Antipas' Digest 3

[The text discussed is Luke 11–12.]

Although you Christians make suspicious claims about Jesus, the quality of your corporate life is impressive, dear Luke, at least if Antonius' community is anything to go by. I met with them for a ninth-hour dinner in honor of their god, Jesus Christ. There I was again treated as a guest when they gathered to enjoy a meal, to observe "the Lord's Supper," and to pray together to god "the father" through Jesus Christ, their benefactor. They asked once again for me to read a section of your monograph on Jesus. Because my voice has been slightly affected by the recent rain, I brought my scribe Glykeros to the gathering for precisely this purpose, and he continued the reading where I had stopped the previous week. Most of those who had gathered the previous week were present, although a few were newcomers.

After the reading, we had a short discussion about what had been read, after which they prayed to and praised Jesus. (I again returned to Euphemos' house prior to their time of prayer and worship.) The whole of our discussion revolved around Jesus' simple words "do not worry" [12:22]. There were two main aspects of our discussion. The first involved Jesus' advice not to be concerned with material things and to sell one's possessions to benefit the poor. I thought that, with this advice, Jesus resembled a Cynic or a Stoic, one who walks strangely through this world as if he does not belong here, forswearing engagement with society except to stand aloof from it as if it were contaminated and to speak against it. Similarly, Jesus' parable about the rich man building up his barns with greater and greater amounts of grain has parallels with Cynic denouncements of those with wealth and status as being foolish and misguided.

It was Demetrius, an outspoken stonemason from Ancyra, whose comment I will have to ponder further. He suggested that, although Jesus the Cynics may have some things in common and share some criticisms of society, they nonetheless differ in their positive proposals. Demetrius thought that, whereas Cynics tend to be individualistic, perceiving the ultimate goal as one's own complete and autonomous detachment from society, Jesus sought relationship with others, creating new configurations of community. (These are my words, of course, but they reflect what I think Demetrius was trying to express. He had been told of Cynic teachings while in Ancyra; the stonemasons' guild there had made every effort to eradicate Cynic influences from the region.) This made sense to me and caused me to rethink my initial impression about Jesus' Cynic credentials. After all, Cynics are not known for valuing their association with others in meal situations, whereas your narrative of Jesus has already suggested that this is a central feature of his life. Moreover, Jesus' attitude toward material possessions emerges from a perspective that envisages a cosmic battle between good and evil, a battle between the empire of the Jewish god and that of his primary opponent, Satan. This conflict is moving toward its final climax, in which the Jewish god will remove from power those who perpetuate the present systems of society and will establish a new empire. To my knowledge, this aspect of Jesus' teaching is unparalleled among the Cynics.

The second thing we discussed in relation to Jesus' advice not to worry is the world of demons. We read a great deal in this section of the narrative about evil spirits, demons, and Satan, the overlord of the cosmic forces of evil. I know of some philosophers who think all of this is simply silly superstition, but they are clearly in the minority throughout our vast empire. In my experience, the populace remains highly fearful and respectful of the suprahuman forces. The spirits of the deceased are powerful, and to tap into those powers can increase one's prospects of success. Magic is one means of harnessing the power of the suprahuman forces through established techniques of incantations and curse formulae. The casting of curses upon competitors and enemies and the attempt to protect oneself against competitors' curses by counter-curses is woven into the fabric of life around the whole of the Mediterranean. Invoking the powers of a deity, an angel, or a departed spirit is a means of manipulating the suprahuman realm in order to accomplish certain purposes within the human realm. Many live their lives in constant fear of the dreaded involvement of evil spirits against their interests. In this context, Jesus' words "do not worry" would have appeared rather unrealistic had you not already depicted him as having the power to exorcise demons and control them. The woman in your narrative who declared a blessing on Jesus' mother [11:27] was presumably comforted by Jesus' claims to overthrow the realm of the demonic [11:14–28].

It was clear to us all that Jesus' advice not to worry was frequently tied to his expectation about a time that is coming when everything will be set right. But Jesus' comments about the coming "judgment" seemed to me to be somewhat old-fashioned. They are typical of the views maintained among many segments of the Jewish population, of course. But the idea that someday we will all stand before the divine tribunal and take account of our lives has little currency among people in my normal circles of life. For my part, I cannot quite see how this old-fashioned notion can be reconciled with the fact that Rome has been established by the gods as an eternal empire, sovereign over all others. Clearly Rome is unconquerable in its supremacy, and the Pax Romana [the peace brought about by Rome] reflects the values of the gods who maintain the empire. If there is a "judgment," it is in the here and now, as the gods honor those who honor them, allowing social miscreants to fall into ruin. Whatever awaits us in the afterlife is simply an extension of what the gods have already organized in this life. But Jesus, like many of his Jewish contemporaries, imagined a single god lying behind all the others, a god whose values are different from, and are frequently contrary to, those of the other gods. This is a curious conviction and in the wrong hands can be used to promote mischief within the empire. Ultimately, however, this curious conviction needs to be tested in light of the undeniable glory, power, and honor of Rome and its gods. I maintain that those of us whom the gods have blessed in this life will continue to curry favor with them in the afterlife.

In this connection, some of us wondered what Jesus was referring to by the term "Son of Man." It is an odd term, and I for one have not been able to make much sense of it. It seems to refer to a divinity who will ultimately judge the whole world. Can you help me and others gathered at Antonius' house to understand the term further?

Luke's Response to Digest 3

Antipas, you are right in your basic understanding of the term "Son of Man," but perhaps you will allow me to add a bit more detail to your current perception, as you yourself have requested.

Part of the problem of the term's oddity can be attributed to the fact that it derives from an ancient text that most Jews include within their scriptures. The book was written by the prophet Daniel. Part of Daniel's book contains a depiction of the course of human history, culminating in the overthrow of societies set up by humans and the ultimate establishment of the empire of Israel's God. In this process of overthrowing illegitimate societies, the Son of Man plays a key role as he engages in battle with a series of beasts [Daniel 7]. These figures—the beasts and the Son of Man—have a representational role, with the beastly figures representing the non-Jewish nations that have ruled in succession. I have never heard any disagreement over this interpretation among Jewish interpreters. There is some dispute, however, over the figure of the human being, the "Son of Man." Most Jewish interpreters seem to think that he represents some kind of angelic figure who comes to earth at the time of judgment when God's ways are established. But Jesus, himself a Jew, seems to have interpreted the figure differently. For him, the Son of Man figure mentioned by Daniel is a representative of God's people Israel in the presence of God—the representative standing between Israel and God. This representative of Israel is ultimately to be given an empire by God, indeed, an everlasting empire that eradicates all other empires. He is to rule over nations and be given divine glory.

You have clearly seen the implication of Jesus' expectation about a coming judgment, even if you were unfamiliar with all the connotations of the term "Son of Man," who in due course will supplant the beastly rulers

in the land. To be sure, Jesus' expectation is at odds with Rome's claim to
be the eternal manifestation of the society of the gods. I do not want to
mislead you. In speaking of the coming Son of Man, Jesus' terminology
carried definite political overtones. Moreover, as my narrative demonstrates, at many points Jesus identified himself as this very figure.
Clearly, this involved an affront to those who work for Rome's glory. In
fact, Jesus' claims to be the Son of Man played a significant part in his
destiny, as my narrative will reveal later. For now, it is enough to suggest
that, although Jesus did not work to the glory of Rome but to the glory
of another empire altogether (that which he called the "empire of God"),
he was not promoting antisocial behavior. He spoke of, lived out, and
died for a message that promotes true health among all people, even if it
did not specifically promote the ways of the empire of Rome. This mixture of challenge and enhancement is what I found to be so distinctive of
him.

Antipas' Digest 4

[The text discussed is Luke 13–14.]

I went back, dear Luke, to meet this week with the Christians gathered in the house of Kalandion. As ever, Kalandion was a gracious host. A noticeable assembly of city officials and noblemen had gathered there on this occasion. Lycomedes and many of his household were present, as were Theodotos (himself a doctor) and Tullia Spendousa, city officials of prominence.

Rufinus was also there. I had not seen him for several weeks, and although he remains a man of study, we have not studied your monograph together for some time. He is rarely seen in the Pergamene acropolis these days, having chanced upon a fortunate association with a senator in Rome and spending much time shoring up that connection. His name is increasingly mentioned in casual temple conversations as one to watch, and he now moves regularly in high-ranking civic circles along with Roman consuls Octacilius Pollio and Claudius Charax. The Pergamenes are hoping he will be a rising figure in Rome, bringing further advancement to the reputation and fortunes of Pergamum and its inhabitants. (I suspect, however, that a few city officials are secretly envious of him and wish him ill, in view of his newfound rise to prominence.) Since he no longer has the luxury of regular study with me, I was glad to see him again. We reclined at dinner together with Lycomedes and others in Kalandion's triclinium, enjoying each other's company and sharing stories of our past. Rufinus' recent advancement in honor has pleased his long-standing friend Kalandion, and those gathered at Kalandion's house seemed to bask in the glow of his presence.

After the dinner, Kalandion asked for a portion of your monograph to be read to the gathering. With my voice recovered, I read the next section. It was not well received. There was a silent embarrassment within the group at some of the narrative, as if Jesus' words were those of a distled crank. Not much was said about large sections of the text. Instead of interest, some passages instilled apprehension among this impressive gathering. Misgivings arose in connection with Jesus' challenge to the system of honor that pervades elite society. For instance, Jesus instructed that there is no point in seeking honor lest the tricky balance of the honor game swing against you [14:7–11]. He followed that with instructions about how to organize a meal: Do not invite your friends, your family, your rich neighbors; instead, invite the poor, the crippled, the lame, and the blind [14:12–14]. There is clearly no honor in any of that, but he offered a vivid story to highlight and emphasize the point further [14:15–24]. I could not help but think of the gathering of Christians who meet at Antonius' house, where this kind of instruction seems to be taken to heart and acted on. At Kalandion's house, however, only a certain sense of nervous discomfort arose as I read Jesus' words.

There was, however, no discomfort when the earlier part of the text was read in which Jesus healed the woman bent over with disease [13:10–17]. That section dominated our discussion, which focused on Jesus' miracle-working power. Jesus was repeatedly praised as Asklepios' emissary. After our discussion, a ritual that imitated a sacrifice was performed in honor of both Asklepios and Jesus, and prayerful requests were made for continued health and prestige.

Throughout the evening, my mind kept returning to those who gathered in the house of Antonius and Mania and how different they were in their understanding of Jesus. In comparison to the gathering at Kalandion's house, the community spirit at Antonius' house is far more intriguing and distinctive. The gathering at Kalandion's house differed little from that of other religious associations in which social advancement is sought through the manipulation of the divinities, and the more divinities the better. Those at the two gatherings are so different in their outlook, values, and lifestyle that it seems strange to apply the label "Christian" to both gatherings. I must ponder these things more.

Dear friend, I was intrigued to read about "the Galileans whose blood Pilate had mixed with their sacrifices" [13:1]. I am unaware of this incident, but I suspect your sources have led you to exaggerate. Surely your portrait of Pilate is somewhat skewed here. He could be a harsh man and at times was heavy-handed in his dealings, but such would be required of any who sought to manage the unruly Judeans with shrewdness and calculated prudence.

LUKE'S RESPONSE
TO DIGEST 4

My friend, Antipas, I must stand by the reliability of my source with regard to Pilate's actions. His prefectship was characterized by numerous brutal episodes, of which the event mentioned in my narrative is only one. You of course know the outline of his political career. After the short and ineffective "reign" of Archelaus, son of Herod the Great, Rome considered it politically expedient to take direct control of Judea. Four prefects had been appointed and removed by Rome in relatively quick succession before Pilate was appointed to what most Romans considered a minor and relatively undesirable provincial assignment. He ruled over Judea at the time when John the Baptist and Jesus of Nazareth were in public view [Pilate's dates of rule are 26–37 C.E.], while Herod Antipas continued to rule over Galilee and Perea.

With the assistance of my scribe, I have managed to locate a description of Pilate recorded by Philo of Alexandria, who describes him as "naturally inflexible, a blend of self-will and relentlessness," given to "briberies, insults, robberies, outrages, and wanton injuries, executions without trial constantly repeated, ceaseless and supremely grievous cruelty" [Philo, *Embassy* 301–2]. This cruel streak in his constitution frequently demonstrated itself in his handling of Jews. Tensions had already been rising between the Jewish people and Pilate's predecessor Gratus, so clearly Pilate inherited a volatile situation. But indicators suggest that Pilate did not concern himself with restoring good relations with those whose lives he controlled in Judea. Even in the very first year of his prefectship, he sent troops carrying images of the emperor into Jerusalem by night. A large crowd of protesting Jews soon besieged his residence in Caesarea demanding the removal of those images. Jewish efforts to negotiate with him came to nothing. Only after an eventual confrontation in the Caesarean stadium did Pilate finally agree to remove the images. But the fact that he undertook this action under the cloak of darkness shows that he knew very well that his actions would infuriate the Jews in the cold light of day. The fact that it took enormous pressure to persuade him to remedy the situation likewise reveals much about his lack of sensitivity toward the Jews.

Added to this insensitivity to Jewish religious sentiment was Pilate's willingness to use brutality rather than diplomacy to accomplish his aims. As is well known, on one occasion, in order to build a new aqueduct, Pilate confiscated the funds from the treasury of the Jerusalem temple— funds intended for the worship of Israel's God. When the Jewish crowds protested this action, Pilate responded by sending soldiers dressed as civilians but armed with clubs into the streets. They injured many and killed some, all with Pilate's blessing. The method was surely cunning; had Pilate sent his troops in normal fashion to quell the protest, it would have been much easier for a Jewish embassy to send an official protest against him to the legate in Syria. Proceeding in the way he did allowed Pilate the opportunity to deny the charge of brutality against the indigenous people because he could simply accuse pro-Roman Jews of taking arms against anti-Roman Jews in the streets without his involvement.

You of course know of the famous event that ultimately resulted in Pilate being recalled to Rome [37 C.E.]. Pilate decided that it was in his interest to block a procession of Samaritans who wanted to ascend Mount Gerizim, their place of worship. This was an affront to the Samaritans and resulted in an armed conflict against Pilate's forces. In the aftermath, Pilate ensured that many Samaritan leaders were executed, including a large number who were not even involved in this particular event. Some Samaritans then appealed for justice to Vitellius, the legate in Syria, and their complaint was considered so significant that Pilate, a Roman citizen and prefect, was sent to Rome for trial.

Consequently, dear Antipas, I think the evidence indicates that, from first to last, Pilate was by no means a fair-minded governor of Judea. On the contrary, on a good many occasions he proved himself to be devious and brutal.

Antipas' Digest 5

[The text discussed is Luke 15–16.]

Having met Antonius in the street earlier in the week, I was invited by him to return to the gathering of Christians who use his house as a base for their weekly meetings. Joining them for the third time, I was again struck by their lack of concern for social codes of honor and shame. Antonius was recognized by all as the patron of the meeting, but he was not treated with the respect ordinarily reserved for one in that position. Or perhaps it is better to say that all the people gathered there were treated with the respect ordinarily reserved for noblemen such as Antonius, a man adorned with every virtue. There was no effort to organize the positions at the meal according to a social hierarchy, and no differences were evident in the kind of food served to those in the atrium and those in the triclinium. (The Jews who prefer a certain level of purity observance ate special food, but this did not disrupt the corporate dynamics significantly.) Some first served food, then they themselves were served. At one point, I even noticed Antonius and Mania delivering platters of fruit and fish to a group comprised of both local artisans and their own household servants. I gather that such is not their regular practice throughout the week, for the servants do function as servants normally. But when they gather as Christians, patterns of behavior are intentionally changed to reflect the fact that members of this group belong to a new order of society, or as they call it, the empire of god. Since I was not treated as a guest this week but as a regular attendee, I felt the expectation to take my turn at serving others, something I have never done before. This was not as humiliating as I would have imagined, most likely because all the others were doing it as well, even Antonius.

After the meal, I again read from your monograph about Jesus, but let me explain what happened at the end of the evening, since I have not previously attended the whole of the meeting. Toward the end of the evening, a young songstress named Kyrilla sang a song of praise to Jesus, accompanied by her small seven-stringed kithara, which she held in her lap. When she had finished, the gatherers created an inventory of needs. Members were encouraged to state any needs they felt unable to meet. This, as I understand it, is something they do regularly in an attempt to extend gestures of goodwill to members of the group and to others throughout the week, as an extension of the "empire" to which they belong. Some spoke of wanting to supply food to some of the expendables on the street; a few were even in need of food themselves. One artisan was concerned about a fellow artisan who had recently become seriously ill, probably because of malnutrition. Then there was the case of Nouna, a young girl of about seven years with brilliant eyes who earlier in the week had simply wandered into the city alone. Until her parents can be found or a suitable arrangement can be made for her, a group of Christians committed themselves to her cause.

These are the sorts of things that were mentioned. Almost all the regular gatherers took responsibility to work with others to meet a need in one way or another. Just as I found myself serving wine to the gatherers earlier in the evening, so I also found myself agreeing to play a role in their inventory. And so it falls to me to ensure that food will be delivered to the ill artisan three times during the coming week. I will have my servant Kyrilos carry out my commitment to that duty.

When gatherers were asked to report on their activities of the previous week, those who were helped by others in the group publicly thanked their helpers, but the helpers did not seem intent on promoting their own reputations. Usually they simply expressed their pleasure in being able to lend assistance, and then they praised their god for his goodness and his caring spirit bestowed on them. No bonds of patronage were established or implied. Assisting others seems to be a normal habit, and those who do so do not expect to receive personal gain in return.

This group of Christians is not simply, as most associations are, an assembly of individuals who share a common interest; instead, its members interact as if they were part of a close-knit family. Not only do they act toward one another in ways that are usually associated with kinship groups, but they also frequently use familial language, calling one another "brother" or "sister" as if their strongest ties of relatedness are to one another, despite their obvious differences. They seem to envisage themselves as members of an empire consisting wholly of family members who care for and support one another.

I also took it upon myself to return to Antonius' house the next day to meet Simon, the Galilean who previously worked for me. He became very ill recently and consequently has been unable to attend the gathering of Christians. Mania mentioned to me during the evening that he would regret having to miss the reading of your monograph about Jesus, and it occurred to me on the following morning that he might appreciate hearing the section that had been read at the gathering. Undeterred by our differences in social rank, I took it upon myself to do this. (Since the act of reading your monograph to the members of the association seems to fall within my orb of responsibility, I therefore felt this private reading to be an honorable task.) Antonius and Mania had gone to attend to their civic duties in the upper marketplace, but I was permitted entry by their household manager. Simon was glad of the company and to hear the text.

The occasion also afforded me another chance to read and discuss an important section of your monograph. The behavior of the Christians at Antonius' house seems to be the natural outworking of some of the things mentioned in this week's reading. The story of Jesus eating with tax collectors and sinners provides the raw ingredients for a community in which normal social codes of honor and shame are considered insignificant. The same is stated explicitly by Jesus, who pronounced the following verdict: "No servant can serve two masters. . . . You cannot serve both God and Money" [16:13]. This divorcing of divine favor and material wealth is standard fare for those disenfranchised within the empire, but it runs contrary to all I have ever believed, that the favor of the gods translates into a status of honor, power, and prestige. The Christians gathered at Antonius' house attribute their efforts of service to the spirit of their god, who is active in their lives. It has nothing to do with a concern to enhance their social reputation. Clearly, they, like Jesus, do not associate divinity with the ingrained standards of honor that pervade the empire. That point was made by one of the traders, Karpos of Ancyra, in relation to Jesus' words, "What is highly valued [within society] is detestable in God's sight" [16:15]. It was also obvious in the intriguing story of the rich man and Lazarus [16:19–31]. The rich man was not blessed by the Jewish god in the afterlife but was said to have transgressed the ways of god by not providing for the needs of others, even those who fell far beyond his world of honor. Of course, this is merely a story, and its validity needs to be tested, for it assumes, again, that some form of radical judgment awaits us after this life. At least Jesus was consistent in defining honor and shame within these parameters rather than those normally associated with the ways of the empire.

As I read to Simon the story of the man with two sons, I realized that he was crying. Images of sons eating the slop of pigs and of daughters forced into prostitution by economic hardship [15:16, 30] cut too close to the bone for him. He worries about the family that he was driven to abandon in the hope of carving out an existence here in Pergamum. Those are feelings and fears that I can barely understand, since my own son thrives in prestigious houses with gem-covered couches, luxurious decor, ornate fashions, and the finest of food and drink. But although I found it difficult to relate to Simon's fears, I somehow felt strangely moved with empathy for him, this peasant and former employee, a man with no education or claim to honor. If Jesus was right to think that status, power, and money are not, in themselves, indicators of divine favor, then perhaps Simon and I have more in common than our social differences would otherwise suggest. It causes me to wonder whether, like the rich man in Jesus' story who was blind to the need that lay at his own gate, I myself have seen the world only in terms of the codes of honor that have been instilled in me since I was a young boy.

I am not convinced that Jesus was right, of course, but I grant you the power of your story and congratulate you on a well-constructed narrative that has enabled me to catch a glimpse of how others might see the world. These things have captured my attention and given me plenty to ponder—precisely what I had hoped for in coming to the learned city of Pergamum. I will continue my study of your narrative and am pleased for the opportunity to relate my musings to the author of such a fine piece of work.[1]

1. Antipas' digest 3 was probably written on 23 April, digest 4 on 30 April (following Stachys' return on 26 April), and digest 5 on 7 May, presumably the same day that the cover letter was composed. These letters were likely sent with Stachys on the morning of 8 May. He would have arrived in Ephesus on the afternoon of 11 May, leaving the following morning to return to Pergamum on 15 May. He returned with Luke's brief letter, recorded below. Luke's responses to digests 3 and 4 were written later, probably between 12 May and 25 May.

A COMPLETE
REVERSAL
OF LIFESTYLE

[No response from Luke has been found corresponding to these texts from Antipas. It is clear from Antipas' next letter (see letter collection 11) that Luke did, in fact, reply; in that letter Antipas mentions information that Luke conveyed to him in his reply. That reply has been lost.]

ANTIPAS' LETTER

Antipas, civic benefactor;

To Luke, friend and scholar;

Greetings.

I have much news to report to you, my friend. I am honored to say that Lycomedes recently asked me to be one of the supervising managers (for as long as I am able) in Pergamum's efforts to remodel its world-famous Asklepion, the temple of Asklepios. Included in my responsibilities will be the addition of a library and the renovation of the interior of the temple. The city of Pergamum is becoming increasingly congested, and the Asklepion itself, as one of the major attractions for those in need of physical cures, is less impressive than it might be. The position was more than likely offered to me in view of my long history of civic benefaction in cities of the empire. It carries a comfortable amount of prestige and honor. I imagine that Euphemos, my kind host who continues to orchestrate profitable scenarios for me, was instrumental in arranging this offer. Lycomedes has assured me that Quadratus and other city officials have given their approval to the suggestion; evidently, they do not see it as in any way distracting from their own prestige. Rufinus' apparent advancement in the eyes of Rome has left significant space for others to advance in his wake, and since I am no longer pursuing career advancement and am still capable of efficient and honorable civic duty, it was thought that I would be perfectly suited to fill this modest role.

Nonetheless, I will not be able to give the project serious attention in the short term, since I have decided to return to Caesarea for some weeks to visit my son and friends there. I have discussed this already with Euphemos, who has promised me a base in his house when I return to Pergamum. I would hope to return late in the summer, before the gladiatorial games. In the meantime, however, I am eager to return to my homeland and renew old acquaintances. I still have some matters of business that will keep me here in Pergamum for a few more weeks, but I envisage bringing these matters to a point of closure in the near future and setting off for Caesarea in mid-June.

In planning my route, I am hopeful that I might find passage on a ship bound for Caesarea departing from your magnificent port of Ephesus. I would come to Ephesus by land and would hope to visit you in the process. The time is ripe to consummate our blossoming friendship by means of a face-to-face encounter. I imagine that I would come to you in mid-June. Will you still be resident at that time in the house of Calpurnius? If a meeting proves inconvenient, you will, of course, let me know. For the next month or so, I will remain in Pergamum, enjoying the company of my new friends here.

Since I last wrote to you, I have continued to provide resources for a poor artisan, as I agreed with the Christians in the house of Antonius. I am also now sponsoring the welfare of Nouna, the young girl whose parents, if they are still alive, seem to have abandoned her. She is an enchanting young girl with deep blue eyes and a voice that sings. She seems to have developed a fondness for Demetrius' wife, Diotis. I provide resources for Nouna, since Demetrius and Diotis do not have the resources to provide for her. They are barren, but with a fondness for children they have become her faithful and loving caregivers. She is thriving under their oversight, unaware of my benefaction. Also, Simon ben Joseph, the Galilean, has slowly but steadily improved. He has been ill for nearly four weeks but is receiving care in Antonius' house. Simon has been present at the weekly gathering of Christians in Antonius' house, and I have also enjoyed his company during my occasional visits to the house of Antonius and Mania. He has an acute sense of humor that has never left him despite his illness.

Stachys looks forward to seeing you. He has taken fondly to his frequent treks between Pergamum and Ephesus and claims to know the road between them as well as he knows the road connecting Caesarea and Tyre. He brings with this letter a gift of thanks and two reports on the reading of your narrative among the Christians gathered at Antonius' house. Perhaps you will find it helpful to learn how your narrative is being read.

May you be blessed.

ANTIPAS' DIGEST 6

[The text discussed is Luke 17–18.]

A chance encounter with Rufinus outside the temple of Isis was very welcome, since the opportunities to enjoy each other's conversation have been decreasing steadily. He told me of plans to build a monument in his favor, so a memorial to L. Cuspius Pactumeius Rufinus might soon be added to the rich historical monuments that adorn the city of Pergamum. He was also keen to hear about my continued reading of your monograph with the Christians at Antonius' house. From this encounter, Rufinus committed himself to attending Antonius' gathering in order to enjoy an occasion for historical study once again. I signaled to him that the gathering at Antonius' house, which he has never attended, is much different from that at the house of Kalandion, but he seemed unconcerned and made arrangements for me to meet him beforehand so that we could make our way to Antonius' house together.

This, of course, seemed an honorable arrangement to both of us, but I fear Rufinus may now think otherwise. Despite my prior warning, he was unprepared for the manner in which Antonius' household operates on occasions when the Christians gather. I fear he was offended by the manner in which codes of honor and social status are moved to the periphery of their gatherings. Granted, almost everyone in attendance knew of Rufinus' increasingly impressive reputation, and several gestures were made to show him due respect. For instance, Antonius ensured that the triclinium was reserved for those who could eat with Rufinus without causing him undue offense, and extra care was exercised whenever people interacted with him. But for the most part the character of the gathering remained as it has always been, and Rufinus seemed well aware that the arrangements for the event did not revolve around the normal patterns of societal behavior.

Rufinus' unease was further compounded by some of the features of your narrative that I have by now come to expect and that he himself has been acquainted with on earlier occasions when we read your monograph together. I imagine that his unease on this occasion was fostered by the dynamics of the gathering in which your text was read. Previously, the somewhat objectionable features of the Jesus narrative may have struck him as mere historical curiosities or the odd musings of a disenfranchised eccentric. In Antonius' house, however, the Christians consider those features to be formative for their assembly. For Rufinus, this was disturbing, especially now that his civic reputation is quickly on the ascent. He found it difficult to countenance Jesus' expansive speech about the empire of the Jewish god. He proved quite vocal in expressing his dissatisfaction with several aspects of the section we read, including the notion that one was held accountable for this life in the next life (something I asked you about previously), the depiction of a Son of Man (a Jewish deity) as a leading figure in that final accounting, and the general assumption that the Jewish god is sovereign over the gods of Rome, when the recent destruction of Jerusalem definitively proved otherwise. Rufinus pointed out that Jesus' parable of the Pharisee and the toll collector [18:9–14] would have its desired effect only with those who felt that those who collect tolls along Rome's extensive roadways are unworthy citizens, whereas in fact they are simply functioning to maintain the good of the empire. And he viewed as naive the assumption that the rich and elite are somehow at odds with the will of the gods.

The person who was most vocal in addressing Rufinus with regard to toll collectors and the elite was Simon, himself a Galilean and a former peasant there. This itself caused Rufinus further aggravation, since he is unaccustomed to being challenged by someone so far below his own station. But Simon spoke with some force and effectiveness, having seen life from the underside, unlike Rufinus. As Simon spoke, I began to imagine more clearly what life must be like for someone in Simon's social position, which would not have been that much different from Jesus' social position, although Simon was a peasant farmer and Jesus was an artisan. I hope to write within the next few days a digest of reflections on Galilean life. This will be a difficult task for me because I have set myself the challenge of writing it from a peasant's point of view, using Simon's experience as the raw data. Our libraries are filled with digests of life from the point of view of the literate elite, but never have I come across a literary artifact documenting the processes of society from a peasant's point of view. If I am able to capture the perspective of a peasant, the finished product would make for a novel and invaluable contribution to any library. If I am able to complete that task, I will include a copy of my work with this digest.

Knowing that Rufinus was uncomfortable in these proceedings, I found a way for us to leave the gathering after the discussion of your monograph, prior to the Christians' worship of Jesus and apportioning of tasks to help others throughout the coming week. As we left, our conversation was somewhat tense. Rufinus was glad I had found a way to exit the proceedings honorably and without shaming Antonius and Mania. But he was also visibly agitated. We departed at his door, whereupon he mentioned our duty to be on guard against societal contamination. I agreed and returned to Euphemos' house, wondering whether Rufinus' reaction indicated an unbalanced understanding of the purposes of your narrative.

Antipas' Historical Reconstruction: Galilean Life from a Peasant's Perspective

The testimony of Simon ben Joseph of Galilee, with additional research from Antipas, son of Philip of Sepphoris and Crateia, civic benefactor and nobleman of Tyre, Caesarea, and Pergamum.

Like most other sectors of society throughout the empire, Galilean society is marked by two tiers of position: those in secure positions and those in insecure positions. Those enjoying a high degree of security are members of the elite, the ruling class and their high-ranking retainers. Those in an insecure situation include the peasants, most artisans and merchants, along with the unclean, the degraded, and the expendables. Although those in secure positions of wealth and power are few in number, they control the majority of the wealth of the society. The elite enjoy an extremely extravagant lifestyle, while the majority of the peasants live the most meager existence.

The elite have the luxury of establishing profitable relationships with other members of the elite, usually facilitated by means of lavish banquets that parade their wealth and opulence in contests of consumption. A member of the elite continually seeks ways of increasing his influence through investment opportunities, business partnerships, patron-client relationships, currying favor with imperial officials, or serving a lucrative ambassadorial function on behalf of his city. An increase in his wealth is a means to increase his power by enlisting the friendship of powerful civic leaders and establishing numerous patron-client networks in which the patron is lauded and praised publicly for his benevolence. The elite portray themselves as favored by the gods and go to great lengths to ensure that the religious institutions of the society promote this claim. Moreover, because the legal system is in their control, they devise laws that will benefit them and work the system of justice in ways that promote their own interests, usually without regard for the effects on the nonelite.

Rural peasants, conversely, expend significant energy simply trying to ensure the survival of themselves and their families. They usually live meager lives at subsistence level, having just enough food and resources to get by. Many fall below that level. Their poor standard of living is not the result of laziness or ineptitude, since a peasant's workday is long and hard. Nor is it the result of poor harvesting techniques, since peasant farmers reap significant gains from agricultural production. Instead, subsistence living is the result of imposed dues, tributes, and taxations, which peasants usually regard as excessively harsh because these expensive burdens extract everything over and above what is required to sustain the peasants' meager existence.

Close ties of kinship provide a small safety net against the hardships of life. The financial setbacks that accompany a poor harvest or other forms of adversity can sometimes be offset through the collective efforts of relatives. Normally, however, if a small landowner experiences a poor harvest caused by drought or some other natural disaster, he finds himself unable to pay his taxes and provide for his family. In cases of this kind, farmers with small tracts of land are forced to borrow money from a member of the elite, usually at high rates of interest. Now the small farmer is in an extremely precarious position and more often than not finds himself unable to repay the loan. Consequently, he is forced to relinquish ownership of the land, as the elite moneylender inevitably forecloses on the loan and instigates a takeover of the peasant farm in repayment of the debt. The elite owner then installs a manager to run the operation, overseeing the harvesting, gathering, and storing of the produce, and exporting it or monetizing it. The manager is expected to extract as much return from the land as possible in order to support the owner's conspicuously extravagant lifestyle in a city far away. The new owner will already have significant tracts of land from which to generate wealth and power, but the acquisition of new land, no matter how insignificant the size, offers a further boost in his unending attempt to ascend the ladder of civic prominence.

In exceptional circumstances, if the elite landowner has connections with senators in Rome or the emperor himself, he may be able to ensure that his lands are excluded from Roman taxation. Frequently, the owner will convert the land to more profitable use. No ordinary peasant, for instance, can join the lucrative wine business, for vineyards require at least four years of growth before producing any kind of return on the initial expenses. An elite owner can afford to wait for the returns and is willing to wait, because the returns are sizable. Consequently, when a member of the elite makes a land acquisition, it is not unusual for vineyards to appear on that land, which had for so long grown grain and other subsistence crops.

The peasant who previously owned the land might be lucky enough to be appointed as a tenant farmer, renting the land he previously owned through a contract regulated by the manager. The tenant farmer is required to meet a high quota of productivity. As long as he is able to do so, he is of use. A failure to meet the quota likely results in a forfeiture of the tenancy agreement. At that point his best hope lies in becoming a slave, in which case he is at the mercy of his owner. Some slave owners treat their slaves reasonably; a slave is property, just as livestock is property, and there are good reasons for ensuring that one's property operates to full efficiency. Nonetheless, many slaves find themselves in situations that provide for nothing other than the most basic requirements of life. They are forced to live together in cramped and squalid conditions and have little to eat. Many are physically abused.

Another option for a tenant farmer who has lost his tenancy is to become a day laborer, hiring himself out at the marketplace to any manager requiring temporary work. For the day laborer, work is sporadic at best, due in part to seasonal fluctuations in workforce requirements, as well as the competition for work among the high number of day laborers seeking to provide scraps of food for themselves and their families. Eventually, due to ill health, poor nutrition, or simply aging, the day laborer is no longer hired for work of any kind and is unable to eke out even the most basic living. His best hope now lies with whatever kin he might have who might be able to provide him with some form of support.

Failing that, he has few options. Some in this position choose to become bandits, taking their chances against those in transit on the roads. Others wander into groups of charismatic religious figures promising a new utopian age. On occasion, some try to fight back against their perceived oppressors, but never with any real degree of success. Most, however, simply end up as beggars on the urban streets, eager for whatever kindly handout comes their way. Most of these options end in an inevitable death. A person in any of these situations has nothing of value to contribute to the machinery that maintains the processes of society and is therefore expendable (if a beggar) or a nuisance (if a bandit or an extremist). He can hope that his offspring will survive somehow, but his daughters more than likely will give themselves to prostitution, and his sons will become slaves or day laborers like their father, with the cycle set to repeat itself all over again. Suicide is not uncommon among those in these dire circumstances.

With these prospects in view, a tenant farmer on a small landholding is always keenly aware of his vulnerable position on the edge of disaster and ruin. His efforts are directed toward staving off the exploitative processes of the elite. He feels constantly oppressed by a combination of excessive financial obligations. First, he must make a payment (of a pre-arranged amount) to the elite landowner by means of the installed manager, who himself expects to receive a sizable contribution for his efforts. Second, he must pay taxes to maintain the fabric of the Roman empire. Such taxes take the form of poll taxes and land taxes, but they are supplemented by toll collections, duties, and tariffs. From a peasant's point of view, taxes of this kind simply line the purses of the elite elsewhere in the empire whose lives of opulence are maintained by means of these excessive tax burdens.

Third, if a Jew, a peasant falls under the burden of an additional tax. Until the destruction of Jerusalem and its temple, this duty came in the form of a temple tax expected from every observant Jewish male in the empire. Temple tribute consisted of a variety of tithings at various times throughout the year. As a result, a sizable amount of agricultural produce was redirected to the temple priests and functionaries. In theory, this tribute was willingly offered as an expression of thanks and devotion to the Jewish god. In practice, these forms of tribute were often given with reluctance because most of the tribute was used to support the extravagant lifestyle of the high priestly clans based in Jerusalem, many of whom purchased their priesthoods in order to reap the significant rewards associated with the position. Their success in amassing wealth from their position is evidenced by the fact that, prior to the destruction of a large sector of the city by Roman forces in the Judean uprising, many of the priestly houses in Jerusalem were comparable in grandeur to the senatorial houses in Rome. Consequently, deep resentment toward the Jerusalem priesthood had taken hold within many sectors of Jewish peasantry prior to Jerusalem's overthrow. Nonetheless, if a peasant farmer was unwilling or unable to pay these temple tributes, he would likely find himself the object of religious ostracism, belittled as a reprobate and one unworthy to remain within the covenant of the Jewish god and the Jewish people. But even if he was viewed with some disdain, his position was nonetheless enviable compared to that of the day laborers and the expendables, whose fate was already decided.

Although the Jerusalem temple has been destroyed, a form of temple taxation has continued for the Jewish people, with taxation revenues now channeled to support the temple of Capitoline Jupiter in Rome. Facing severe financial difficulties and with the Jerusalem temple no longer in existence, the emperor Vespasian [emperor 69–79 C.E.] decided to redirect into the Roman coffers the tribute money that had formerly been paid to the Jerusalem temple. (Such an act simultaneously punishes the Jewish people for their uprising and insults their pretensions to independence.) A tax of two denarii for each of the five million Jews of the empire is now required to support the Roman Capitoline temple. A tax that had previously been offered in support of the Jewish god is now conscripted to promote the high god of the Roman empire.

ANTIPAS' DIGEST 7

[The text discussed is Luke 19–20.]

Despite Rufinus' warning about social contamination, I returned to the house of Antonius and Mania, since I have entered into an implicit pact to study your narrative with them, perhaps even to ensure that the deficiencies of Jesus' views are pointed out to them. I am pleased that Rufinus was not among our number this week because your narrative, honorable friend, continues to suggest that Jesus stood in opposition to some currents of society.

A case in point is your story about Zacchaeus [19:1–10], the chief toll collector whose encounter with Jesus resulted in uncharacteristic behavior for one in his position: He decided to give away half of his possessions to the poor and repay any injustices at four times the amount. Toll collectors are not likely to act in the manner advocated by Zacchaeus. They usually pay a significant amount to gain their position and then might recoup their losses by levying duty and taxes on merchants and travelers passing by on the road they oversee. They may be despised by the majority of the people, but the lucrative aspect of the position makes it attractive to those willing and able to undertake it. For Zacchaeus to undertake financial recompense on behalf of the poor and oppressed indicates a complete reversal of lifestyle and motivation on his part as a consequence of his encounter with Jesus. That, of course, is what we have come to expect from your narrative about Jesus, who advocated a lifestyle at odds with normal expectations.

In light of this, those of us gathered at Antonius' house debated Jesus' meaning with regard to paying taxes to Caesar: "Give to Caesar what is Caesar's, and to God what is God's" [20:25]. We found that this ambiguous saying could be interpreted in two different ways. It could simply mean that taxes should be paid to the emperor. Give the emperor his due.

129

This is how I initially heard Jesus, because the emperor is known as the representative of the gods here on earth, and the bounty of the empire is determined by the emperor's favor with the gods. Demetrius suggested, however, that perhaps Jesus had constructed a shrewd answer that had another meaning altogether. After all, many Jews consider their god to be the high god and the only god worthy of worship. For them, the emperor is not a representative of the gods here on earth. Perhaps, then, as Demetrius suspected, Jesus had devised a clever way to set the demands of his god above the system of life within the Roman empire. Jesus seems not to have been carrying a denarius, so perhaps he had already chosen to withdraw from that system. His reply might have been a challenge to the honor of the spies sent to question him, since they remained immersed in the finances of the empire. This would also explain why the spies were astonished by Jesus' answer. If he had simply meant to say, "Yes, pay tribute to the emperor," there would be little reason for astonishment. Presumably, then, Jesus' statement was, as Demetrius suggested, yet another challenge to the system driven by the empire, albeit in a cleverly constructed fashion.

If Jesus challenged the ways of the empire, he also seemed to position some of the leaders of the Jewish people firmly within the cultural ethos of the empire. He described them in a manner that would apply to most members of the elite throughout the empire: They seek public respect and praise, expect civic honors, and swoop in to take personal advantage of vulnerability in others wherever it is to be found [20:46–47]. In this way, the leaders of the Jewish way of life were depicted as being fully immersed in the system of honor and shame that permeates the culture of the empire. Perhaps this explains something of Jesus' surprising actions in the temple, where he attempted to drive out those who were involved in business there [19:45].

In view of Jesus' teachings and actions, it is no surprise to me that he was eventually crucified by those in power, as you have already indicated to me and is clear from the Christian gatherings. What is surprising is that it did not happen sooner, but perhaps that is because Jesus spent most of his time in Galilee rather than in Jerusalem, the epicenter of political life in Judea. When Jesus entered Jerusalem, the stakes seemed to rise in the conflict between the elite and powerful leaders of the Jewish people and the poor, rural artisan Jesus. Jesus often directed harsh and critical words at their practices and values and supported his criticisms with the belief in one's final accountability before a god who stands opposed to the ways of the world [20:47]. Your narrative unsurprisingly explains that the chief priests of the temple, the teachers of the law, and the leaders among the people looked for a way to arrest him [20:19]. Yet it also makes a distinction between the elite Jewish leaders and the ordinary Jewish people, who found attraction in what Jesus stood for [19:48; 20:19]. This only reinforced the problem that Jesus posed for the leaders, since they found their authority undermined by this peasant artisan from Galilee. Little wonder, then, that their desire to remove him from the scene sometimes led to an outright desire to kill him [19:47].

If your information is correct, Jesus rightly predicted the destruction of Jerusalem by the unrelenting forces of Rome [66–70 C.E.; see 19:42–44]. For Jesus, the impending destruction of Jerusalem seems to have been another indicator that the most fundamental pillars of the Jewish way of life were embroiled in patterns of life that ran contrary to the will of the Jewish god. This intriguing interpretation radically reverses the common interpretation of recent events. Instead of seeing the destruction of Jerusalem as an indication of the weakness of the Jewish god before the mighty gods of Rome, Jesus interpreted that event (ahead of time) as an indication of the sovereignty of the Jewish god, who opposes those whose practices are in conflict with his desires. For Jesus, the temple's eventual destruction by Roman forces was not a sign of the triumph of Rome's god over Israel's god but simply indicated that the Jewish god had grown displeased with his temple functionaries. In this way, your narrative manages to retain the honor of the Jewish god in the light of recent events.[1]

1. Dates for the preceding correspondence would seem to be as follows: Digest 6 was written on 14 May; digest 7 was written on 21 May; Antipas' historical reconstruction of Galilean life from a peasant's perspective was written between those two dates; Antipas wrote the cover letter on 21 May and sent Stachys to Ephesus on 22 May; Stachys arrived in Ephesus on 25 May, departing on 26 May and arriving back in Pergamum on 29 May.

A CONDUIT
OF BLESSING
FOR MANY

[No reply to Antipas' correspondence has been found. If Luke did reply, his letter has been lost.]

ANTIPAS' LETTER

Antipas, benefactor;

To Luke, friend and scholar;

Greetings.

The time is fast approaching when I will be leaving Pergamum to travel back to my home, and I am very much looking forward to what lies ahead. To be reunited with my son and former associates will please me greatly. I will take only a few of my servants with me in order to travel with greater ease; my son's household in Caesarea will provide me with an abundance of servants when I arrive there. Only Stachys; Herminos, my personal servant; and Attikos, my administrator and scribe, will accompany me during the land travel and sea voyage.

Simon the Galilean will join me on the journey as a travel companion. We may not be ideally suited as travel companions, since we have quite different standards of lifestyle and move in different social circles. Moreover, his concern to practice a Jewish lifestyle will require attention at every point. Nonetheless, we will be amicable travel partners. Our encounters at the house of Antonius have been the spark to light a fire of friendship—a term not ideally suited to two such as us, marked out as we are by an obvious disparity in our social stations. But Simon seems not to think of me as an oppressive landowner, as many peasants might, and he holds no grudge against me for my invisible and unknowing part in his hardships. He even dares to call me "brother" in the gathering of Christians at Antonius' house (although I find I cannot reciprocate). For my part, although his ways are clearly not those of the refined elite, I find Simon to exude an infectious zest for life to a degree that is inexplicable in relation to the difficulties he has experienced. Despite our many differences, we have found a common bond in two important features: First, our deeply rooted affections lie in the eastern Mediterranean, where our identities were nurtured and developed; second, we are both fathers separated from our families.

And so we plan to travel together for most of the journey. Once we reach Caesarea, I will establish myself in my familial residence. Simon will then travel to Galilee to seek out whoever remains of his family. In our travels, he will be my associate, sponsored by Antonius, with his own letter of recommendation. He is excited at the prospect of returning to Galilee, although in the near future he is required to rest; his recovery from illness took far too long, and he still has not regained his full strength.

I have put into motion some of the foundational processes for the rebuilding of the Asklepion. The building plans have already been submitted and approved (something that took place prior to my appointment as a supervising manager), so I was able earlier this week to begin the process of conscripting managers to oversee the variety of tasks that require attention. While I am away, two managers will begin assembling workforces and acquiring the extensive materials required for the project in the hopes that work might begin in earnest as soon as possible. I am keen to restore the Asklepion to its former glory. Since its construction, it has been overshadowed by the marvelous Pergamene temples to gods other than Asklepios, not least Athena, Zeus, Helios, Dionysus, Demeter, and Hygieia. Perhaps the Pergamene Asklepion will again rival the Asklepia of other cities, such as Kos [the main city on the island of Kos], Rome, Athens, Corinth, and of course Epidauros.

Meanwhile, little Nouna is beginning to thrive. She is the joy of our weekly gatherings and has managed to creep into my heart in a very short period of time. She has taken to acting out stories of Jesus, to our great delight. Her favorites seem to be Jesus' parables, including the Pharisee and the toll collector [18:9–14], the ten minas [19:11–27], and the tenants in the vineyard [20:9–19]. She sometimes muddles up the details of the parables, but what is lost in accuracy is gained in endearment. We have made arrangements to establish her permanently with Demetrius and Diotis. I have ensured that they are granted a financial contribution each month to provide for her needs, and they are playing their part in providing her with a caring environment. I will miss her when the time comes for me to journey to Caesarea.

Plans are also now being laid for the second gladiatorial event of the year in the late summer. I have sent word to Rufinus about my intended journey to Caesarea, with my apologies for not being available to lend assistance in the organization of this event, as I did for the last one. I regret that my plans do not permit my involvement in the organization, since there is a rumor that the emperor himself might attend. I intend to return to Pergamum in time to attend, however. Rufinus will be well served by Kalandion, whose involvement in the last event no doubt prepared him well for more responsibility in this one.

I greatly look forward to meeting with you in person in a very short while. Our friendship has grown from pleasantries shared among equals to frank interaction on issues of significance. I am sure that my visit will only enhance the benefits that have already come my way as a result of our association. When I see you in person, we can arrange for me to receive a copy of the second volume in your monograph of Jesus and his followers. Perhaps it would be most opportune for me to start reading that volume with the gatherers at Antonius' house upon my return to Pergamum.

I also look forward to meeting Calpurnius, of course. I was pleased to hear your news of his safe return [Luke's letter in which this was reported has not been found], and I hope to hear more about his travels when I am with you.

Stachys will relate to you my intended movements for the first part of the journey so that you will not be caught off guard by our visit.

My wishes for your health and blessing precede me.

ANTIPAS' DIGEST 8

[The text discussed is Luke 21:1–22:62.]

I again joined the Christians who meet at Antonius' house and was entertained most of the time by young Nouna, whose antics have cast a spell over me. She insisted to Mania that she distribute the bread to everyone. Unable to carry a bread basket herself, she then conscripted me as her servant, a role I was to play for most of the dinner, carrying the basket behind her while she made sure that everyone had his fill. In the process, she renamed me so that I became Stachys, and she took my name, Antipas. This was harmless fun. I teased her by saying that, in Jesus' view, I, as the servant, was greater than she, the master, since the last will be first, and the first will be last [13:30]. Our role playing concluded toward the end of the meal, when she became tired and fell asleep in Diotis' arms.

After dinner, we assembled in the courtyard of Antonius' house, and I read again from your monograph. We noted several things. First, we were puzzled by Jesus' instruction that his followers should carry swords [22:36–38], although when one of them used his sword against the servant of the high priest, Jesus put a stop to that kind of action. It would be interesting to know which follower made use of the sword. Demetrius thinks he heard that it was Peter [cf. John 18:10], who is soon to swing to the other extreme of reaction and betray Jesus. Simon thought there might be some irony in the fact that, when Judas and his company approached Jesus and his disciples, they were met with a sword. Simon holds the view that Judas was named Iscariot [22:3] as a play on the word *sicarii,* the daggermen. If so, this would identify him as a member of the extreme factional group of daggermen who kidnapped and murdered prominent Jewish aristocracy as punishment for their compliance with Rome, and who maintained that the Jewish god alone is sovereign and should reign over the Jews. But I pointed out that Simon's theory is based on the assumption that the sicarii group existed in Jesus' day, which is not necessarily the case. I did not hear of their existence until a few years prior to the Jewish uprising against Rome [66–70 C.E.]. Moreover, as Simon admitted, the name "Iscariot" could simply mean "man from Kerioth," Kerioth being a Judean village.

Several features of this reading were reminiscent of issues mentioned earlier in your monograph. Jesus continued to highlight the final judgment by the Son of Man [21:27, 36], whom Jesus interpreted as himself, the one who suffers [22:20–22]. Again Jesus predicted the destruction of Jerusalem, stating that the city would be "surrounded by armies" and "trampled on by the gentiles" [21:20, 24]—events that happened as he predicted.

Moreover, Jesus continued to invert societal norms, chiding those of us who take pride in our long-standing public benefaction and extolling the virtues of powerlessness [21:1–4; 22:24–30]. I expressed some resistance to this sentiment. Without benefactors to promote the social and material fabric of society, the empire would come to a grinding halt, collapsing into chaos and anarchy. Demetrius had a different view. He thought that the problem did not lie with Jesus' vision but with the fact that his vision had been grasped by only a minority of people. He imagined that if the whole world were to live by Jesus' vision, there would be no need for the system of benefaction as currently practiced by the elite. The problem with benefaction, in his view, is the way it promotes the public honor of a benefactor engaged in an intricate contest for prestige and power. The need to acquire additional material resources in order to exemplify the benefactor's power and honor usually causes him to take predatory advantage of the vulnerable in an unrelenting and exploitative manner. (At this point, I wanted to object, but I was conscious of Simon's presence in the meeting and knew that his situation in Galilee resembled what Demetrius had described. I found it impossible to turn my gaze toward Simon.) Benefaction itself may not be the problem, Demetrius suggested; the problem lies with the larger system of honor and shame in which benefaction operates.

I mentioned in reply that the practice of those who gather at Antonius' house of caring for others in need might itself be considered a form of benefaction. But Simon felt that this kind of benefaction differs from the kind denounced by Jesus, in which benefactors lord their positions over others in a bid to inflate their own reputations. Simon felt that Christians were expected to engage in acts of kindness only to enhance the reputation of their god, in the expectation that he would look favorably on those acts and use them as vehicles of blessing. This, he felt, was how his god had used Jesus' act of kindness. Jesus' death on behalf of others became a conduit of blessing for many who find that even their insignificant lives are valued in the eyes of their god.

These views are difficult to adjudicate. What is clear from your narrative is that Jesus expected those who live by his vision to meet with opposition within the empire. This is not surprising, of course. He is realistic about his own fate, and he is also well aware of the fate that might await those who honor him. He contrasted the cares of this world [21:34] with obedience to his god, and he demonstrated obedience in accepting what he perceived as his divinely ordained calling. At the same time, he expected that his followers would be persecuted by kings and governors for their lifestyles [21:12].

The theme of persecution sparked off an interesting discussion about Christians who have already been persecuted. For instance, mention was made of the Christians who were set alight in the circus of Rome under instructions by Nero, about which you and I have already corresponded. I remembered your comment that the Peter depicted in your narrative was executed for his convictions. What an irony, then, that the one who denied Jesus three times went on to die as a martyr for Jesus' cause. Perhaps the rest of your narrative explains his transformation.

In relation to Peter's denial of Jesus, Photion, one of our number, reported that those who meet in the house of Kalandion have now decided to disband their meetings at Kalandion's house and move their gatherings to the temple honoring Rome and Augustus, the first provincial temple for a Roman emperor in all of Asia Minor. They expect to gather there regularly on the Lord's Day so that it will be clear to all that their worship of Jesus does not conflict with their worship of other gods. Evidently, the impetus for this adjustment came from a warning from Rufinus, who sees the worship of Jesus to be troublesome for Pergamum's fortunes in the eyes of the empire. Domitian's claim to divinity is nonnegotiable, and the priests of the imperial cult expect worship of the emperor to be incorporated into the fabric of everyday life. Consequently, those at Kalandion's house have decided to signal their status as honorable citizens of the empire by worshiping the powerful Jesus within the imperial temple itself.

Photion wondered whether this was simply common sense or whether, in fact, it amounted to a subtle form of betrayal, like that of Peter. To me, it seems a strategically sensible move for that gathering of Christians. Nonetheless, I see that it could not be adopted as a strategy for those gathering at Antonius' house without shattering the delicate ethos of their corporate life. I mentioned that any who wish to worship the emperor could easily do so in the imperial temple at any point in the week. The gatherings at Antonius' house, therefore, are not necessarily in conflict with the wishes of the emperor. Nonetheless, I am aware that some strong-minded Christians at Antonius' house would not be eager to offer sacrifices to the emperor, since they consistently affirm their conviction that Jesus himself is the incarnate form of the creator god, who alone is worthy of worship. Still, I considered it prudent to mention the option, if only to plant the seed of the idea. Nothing was said in response. The prospect of the emperor's escalating demands to be worshiped seemed to create an unexpressed sense of foreboding among some of the gatherers.

At this point, Demetrius suggested that perhaps "persecution" should not be defined only with reference to martyrdom. As a stonemason, he is finding it increasingly difficult to carry out his trade. The stonemasons' guild prides itself in honoring the emperor, and its meetings include the offering of sacrifices to the emperor. Guild membership fees have been increased to include a donation to the imperial temple in order to promote the worship of the emperor in Pergamum. The guild exercises such power within the city that stonework is available only to its members. Demetrius is a member of the Pergamene guild, just as he was in Ancyra, but he is also known as a worshiper of Jesus, so he is looked upon with some suspicion. Recently, work has not been quick in coming to him because he does not support emperor worship and therefore is suspected of neglecting his civic duties. Being a follower of Christ has had an impact on his economic situation. Perhaps this is a form of persecution.

Two other stonemasons feared that something similar might happen to them. They admitted that Peter's act of denying his allegiance to Jesus had some economic attraction in the present climate, but they also noted Peter's sorrow over having betrayed his master. They thought it beneficial to their own situation that Kalandion and other prominent citizens are known to worship both the emperor and Christ. As a consequence, being known as a Christian does not necessarily indicate to others one's attitude toward emperor worship. As long as these signals are given out, perhaps the reputation of Christians will not degenerate further, and worshipers of Jesus can quietly carry out their work without penalty.

Antipas' Digest 9

[The text discussed is Luke 22:63–24:53.]

At the most recent gathering of Christians at the house of Antonius, I read the final section of your monograph on Jesus the Galilean. This section is a fitting climax to the narrative—full of political drama, intrigue, and pathos, capturing personal moments set against a larger backdrop of history and presenting the reader with the significance of the central protagonist in an implicit manner. In the past three months, when enjoying your monograph at a leisurely pace, I have found you to be a most capable author, and again I commend you for having constructed a most compelling narrative from sources at your disposal.

After reading the text, I could not help but think that your depiction of Jesus' crucifixion might have been far more graphic in detail. I wonder, in fact, whether you have brought out the horrors of crucifixion to the extent that you might have. It is, as you know, my friend, a most excruciating manner of death, and for that reason Roman officials use it as one of their preferred forms of execution for enemies of the empire. The horror starts with the severe scourging of the victim with a flagellum. The flogging is permitted to continue to the satisfaction of the one doing the scourging; there is no limit to the number of lashings a Roman soldier can inflict. I have heard of victims who have not survived this stage in the proceedings, their flesh having been ripped off down to the bone by the bits of rock and hooks tied to the end of the thongs. If Jesus required assistance in carrying his crossbar, as your narrative suggests,[1] and if he died so quickly after having been placed on the cross, presumably he had lost an inordinate amount of blood prior to his crucifixion, suggesting that his lashings had been of the most severe kind. You spared your reader

---

1. Usually the victim was forced to carry his own crossbar; cf. John 19:17. For Jesus needing assistance in carrying the crossbar, see also Mark 15:21; Matt. 27:32.

any mention of this, as well as any mention of the driving of long nails into Jesus' wrists and ankles, which is the part of the proceedings that most horrifies me. Presumably Jesus died, as most crucifixion victims do, of suffocation, as exhaustion set in and his body collapsed on itself, unable to support itself in a manner that permits proper breathing. In the eyes of the protectors of social stability, his death would have helped to instill fear in those who would contemplate acting in a manner that undermines the empire.

But your narrative seems to suggest that Jesus did not fit well within the category of social revolutionary. Even here in the final section of your text, you seem concerned to demonstrate on the one hand how Jesus challenged central features of society (whether Roman or Jewish) and on the other hand how his interests and aims stood in stark contrast to those of revolutionaries. Prior to Jesus' death, Pilate deemed him innocent of social unrest [23:4, 14–16, 22]. A Roman centurion also identified him as an innocent man after seeing his manner of death [23:47]. And an honorable member of the elite, Joseph the Arimathean, who had access to Pilate, found Jesus to be an honorable man and worthy to be treated as such in burial, providing him with an honorable burial [23:50–54]. Evidently, then, Jesus, a challenger of the system, found favor not merely with the peasantry, as one might expect, but also with noblemen. Perhaps Jesus found favor also in the eyes of the nobleman Theophilus, Calpurnius' father, who commissioned your monograph.

In some ways, it is Herod Antipas, the tetrarch of Galilee and friend of the emperor Tiberius, who emerges from your narrative somewhat unfavorably. I have shared his name all my life and inherited from my father, Philip, a great respect for Antipas. His many contributions to life in Galilee include the Romanization of the region and his vast and impressive building projects. The most magnificent in scope include his building of the city Tiberias and his rebuilding of the city Sepphoris, or Autocratoris (now also called Neronia). The names of those cities reflect his attempts to honor the emperor with flattery,[2] just as his father, Herod, had flattered Caesar Augustus when naming Caesarea. But in your narrative, Herod Antipas seems to miss the larger dynamics of what is transpiring before him, seeing Jesus merely as a means to gratify his own desire for entertainment. In some ways, he reminds me of the Pergamene Chris-

2. Tiberias was, of course, named after the emperor Tiberius; "Autocratoris" is related to the Greek equivalent of the Latin "Imperator," an imperial title established in Augustus' time.

tians who met at the house of Kalandion. They seem attracted to Jesus merely because he is able to perform wonders on their behalf. It seems that Herod Antipas' somewhat deficient perception of Jesus' significance has its contemporary counterparts.

Some of us were of the opinion that you portrayed Pilate as one who sought to act justly in the case of Jesus. That may well be. But I also pointed out that, as you recently outlined for me, Pilate was something of a ruthless prefect whose actions were frequently unrestricted by the canons of common justice. I wondered whether other motivations might have been involved in his handling of Jesus' case. I suggested, for instance, that Pilate might initially have intended simply to insult the Jewish leaders by finding Jesus innocent, whereas they along with the rest of the people had found him offensive. Instead of accepting the insult and permitting themselves to be shamed, the Jewish leaders devised a way to put added pressure on Pilate by implicitly threatening him with a scenario that would have brought shame to him: the request for the release of the insurrectionist Barabbas. Their request involved an implied threat that they, members of the elite who normally worked to maintain social stability through collaboration with Rome, would side with political insurrectionists if Pilate failed to grant their wishes in Jesus' case. The stakes were raised, and Pilate's position became unstable. The leaders had subtly indicated to Pilate that he had only one option: comply with their desire to remove Jesus from the scene. If Pilate shamed them by releasing Jesus against their wishes, they would resort to shaming Pilate by permitting nationalistic sentiment to be stirred up among the throngs of pilgrims in Jerusalem who had gathered for the Passover. Simon reminded us of the political significance of this festival, a celebration in which thousands of Jews from all over the empire converged on Jerusalem to celebrate their liberty from Egyptian domination long ago. Clearly Pilate, the representative of Roman domination, had cause for concern. The last thing he needed during a festival celebrating Jewish national independence was for the Jewish leaders to stir up trouble. Better to appease the leaders on this occasion than to lose their collaboration in securing peace in a volatile context. And so, ironically, the prefect of Roman rule was forced to free an enemy of Roman rule. Threatened with a situation of shame, the Jewish leaders managed to keep their honor intact by implicitly threatening Pilate; faced with his own potentially shameful situation, Pilate too managed to keep his honor intact by acquiescing to the Jewish leaders' demands. The only one whose honor was not maintained was Jesus, who carried the shame of crucifixion. The shaming of the crucified man, Jesus, preserved the honor of the other players.

The events described in your narrative regarding the Jerusalem temple are suggestive. You narrate how the curtain of the temple was torn in two and the sun stopped shining [23:45]. We discussed what these events might imply. The combination of dramatic events in both the temple and the natural order suggests that the god who dwells in the Jerusalem temple is also sovereign over the forces of nature. Your narrative has made this claim repeatedly in various ways. But what is not quite as clear is what the tearing of the temple curtain itself signifies. If the gods have emotions (as Homer clearly thinks), the torn curtain might reflect the extreme emotion (perhaps sorrow or rage) of the god whom Jesus called "father." But this did not seem to be your point. We wondered whether the torn curtain signaled that the god of the Jews had abandoned his temple dwelling. If so, this might signify that the god of Israel chose not to preside over the death of Jesus from the environs of the Jewish temple but from the environs of his heavenly temple as the sovereign of the world.

This interpretation is attractive because it coheres with your implicit claim that Jesus' death had universal significance. It also coheres with what I noted previously with regard to Jesus' prediction of the temple's destruction. He did not attribute that future event to Rome's almighty power but to the dissatisfaction of Israel's god with the Jewish temple leadership. The torn curtain might reinforce the same point. The god of the Jews had not acted to protect his Jerusalem temple against the Roman troops that later attacked it because he had already left its precincts. In that case, Rome cannot claim the subjugation of Judea as an indicator of the supremacy of its gods over the god of Israel—a significant interpretation of recent events and one worthy of your intriguing monograph.

If this is your point, it is interesting that the narrative ends where it began—in the temple, with the disciples praising their god there. Apparently, the implications of the tearing of the temple curtain have yet to dawn on them; their god resides in that temple no longer. Where, then, does he reside? Presumably, Jesus' disciples discover the answer to that question in the sequel you have written. Demetrius claimed that the one whom Jesus called father resides in communities where the spirit of Jesus is evident, even in the lives of those who gather at Antonius' house to worship Jesus. This is a curious notion, which seems to me to confuse the sacred world of the numinous with the ordinariness of the everyday world.

When I pointed that out to him, he agreed and said that he meant to say precisely what I noted. He has very firm beliefs, as you can see! But it strikes me as unusual to see the ordinary as the vehicle for the divine. This merging of sacred and ordinary takes place in the inner sanctuaries of temples and in the person of the emperor Domitian (as claimed by the priests of the imperial cult). For that mixture of the divine and the ordinary to occur even in the lives of common laborers is a radical notion, but again it would not be out of place in a radical narrative such as yours.

Clearly, the punch of your narrative comes at the very end, with the resurrection of Jesus and his ascension into the heavenly world. These acts seem to be more than a simple vindication of one who claimed to act on behalf of his god. They reveal that Jesus can fill the role he predicted for himself—that of the ultimate and sovereign judge of the world, the Son of Man exalted to the right hand of the mighty god. I noted that this provided the narrative with a fitting point of closure, with the resurrection of Jesus highlighting the point he had made throughout his life: Jesus' god chooses the weak and the despised as the favored vehicles of divine power and mercy. That a crucified outcast is resurrected by divine power is itself a most dramatic example in the theology of reversal that Jesus espoused throughout his life.

A debate ensued regarding whether these stories of resurrection and ascension simply served to end the narrative with an appropriate closure, as I initially presumed, or whether they have a historical basis, as Demetrius and others argued. I suspect we were not the first to consider this matter, nor the last.[3]

3. The following dates are likely for these texts. Antipas wrote digest 8 on 28 May and digest 9 on 4 June. He also wrote the cover letter on 4 June, sending Stachys to Ephesus on 5 June. Stachys arrived at Calpurnius' house on 8 June, departing on 9 June and arriving back in Pergamum on 12 June.

THE GODS HAD
OTHER PLANS

[No replies to Antipas' letters from Antioch and Caesarea have been found.
It is unlikely that Luke or Calpurnius responded, given that Antipas was in
transit and seemed to expect no reply to these letters.]

ANTIPAS' FIRST
ANTIOCH LETTER

Antipas, traveling nobleman and citizen;

To Luke, scholar and friend, and to Calpurnius, nobleman of Ephesus;

Greetings.

I am writing to you from Antioch in Syria, on the Orontes River, where our travels have brought us through an unfortunate turn of events. Simon and I benefited greatly from your hospitality. We were refreshed by your resources and enormously enjoyed our conversations together. The opportunity to meet you both in person only increased my affections for you. Your efforts to place us on board the ship *Isis* were greatly appreciated, and we left the port of Ephesus in high spirits, bound for Caesarea Maritima. We had expected that, upon arriving in Caesarea, Simon would stay in my household for a few days before journeying with one of my servants as an assistant to discover the whereabouts of his family members in Galilee (with his letter of recommendation from Antonius standing him in good stead). But the gods had other plans, evidently, and disaster struck, with Simon becoming the victim of Fate's cruel hand. He is currently being attended to by Christians here in Antioch, the second time that Christian hospitality has been offered to him in desperate times. But whereas Antonius was able to nurse him back to health in Pergamum, I fear that this time might be different for him. He is desperately ill. You will want to offer prayers for his health, as I am. He has become a trusted friend in our brief time together, and our mutual travels have reinforced our bond of friendship. Although not a nobleman by birth or stature, he has a noble spirit, along with a giving heart and an enthusiastic zeal. Perhaps the gods will look kindly on him, especially the god of Jesus Christ, who gave his life for the sake of others.

The situation arose in this way. We departed from Ephesus in favorable conditions, with bright sunshine, blustery winds, and high hopes of arriving in Caesarea within five or six days. The wind was behind us, and all looked set for a steady progress. The master of the ship had sacrificed to the gods in the morning, and during the previous night neither he nor his ship hands had had any dreams that could be interpreted as bad omens. The ship was a cargo ship, but alongside our small entourage were others who had also acquired passage on the ship. Most were noblemen who could afford to pay for the voyage, but there were also a few couriers delivering messages or goods to their masters' associates elsewhere in the empire. Also on board was a young woman, calling herself Galatia, poorly clothed, with few resources, and having to care for a baby girl. She had probably spent most of her resources simply to pay for their passage. The food she had brought on board was barely enough to keep them for three days. Galatia seemed content to stay by herself with her baby and never explained her circumstances. Simon suggested to me that she was probably a slave fleeing from a harsh master. She seemed uncertain as to where she was traveling but was clearly eager to move on.

The first two days of our travel passed without event. By the evening of the second day, however, things were soon to change. We erected our canvas shelters and bedded down for the night. Galatia and a few others who did not have the means to purchase a shelter settled into their bedding at various points around the deck. The evening seas were tranquil. After only two or three hours of sleep, however, the sea became noticeably rough. The wind picked up, and the moon was covered by a thick blanket of cloud. Soon the strong winds gave way to a howling gale that threw the waves upon us and spit down a fierce rain. The ship hands, having been lulled into a false sense of security by the calm conditions at the start of the evening, had drunk themselves into a stupor and were ill prepared to adjust the sails with the onslaught of the elements. They had lashed the ropes of the mainsail to the blocks. Time after time we tried to release the ropes but to no avail, for they had been swollen by the rain and stubbornly refused to be adjusted. If we attempted to cut the ropes, we would risk dropping the sails into the sea like an anchor, causing the ship to capsize. Unable to shorten the sails, we charged along under full canvas at a fearful speed. We had a double fear: fear of being engulfed by the sea, and fear of being dashed upon

the rocks, for we had no idea of our course or location. We were all terri-
fied and called upon the gods to remember us or, if we died, to remember
our dear ones. One passenger handed out pieces of string, urging us to tie
our jewelry and gold around our necks so that, were our bodies found, the
finders could profit from the find and would not be adverse to disposing
of our corpses in an honorable fashion. These conditions continued throughout the next day and well into the next night. We were exhausted, and what
energy we did have was consumed by the shivering of our bodies as they
tried to offset the cold of the driving winds and waves that had soaked our
clothes to the skin. Then, in the dead of the night, the storm seemed to end
almost as quickly as it had come upon us.

As day broke, we met the sun's first rays with the greatest of relief. The
heat of the sun caused the ropes to dry and shrink just enough to enable us
to adjust and control the sails. The master of the ship was uncertain of our
location, but two hours after sunrise we spotted land. As we sailed closer
to it, the master recognized it as the northeastern tip of the island of Cyprus.
The storm had pushed us northeastward, between Pamphylia and Cyprus.
The master decided to abandon Caesarea as a destination and headed instead
for Antioch, only a day's journey away, where necessary repairs could be
made to the ship.

During the day, many of us slept to regain something of our strength.
By the afternoon, Simon looked feeble and pallid. I expressed concern
for his health, but he brushed the matter aside in an attempt to appear
animated. One or two others were also showing signs of exhaustion. Galatia's baby cried most of the day. Simon and I gave the mother some of the
bread we had brought along that had not been soaked by the storm. At
one point in the afternoon I felt the girl's forehead, and it was very hot.
When the coolness of the evening came upon us, the baby settled down
into a restless sleep. I said good night to my friends and servants and went
to sleep. I awoke in the morning to find that Simon had not slept in his
shelter, having insisted that Galatia and her baby make use of it while he
slept elsewhere on deck. Galatia awoke refreshed, and her baby's fever had
broken in the night, suggesting that she would recover. Simon, on the
other hand, was noticeably worse after being exposed to the night in a
weakened condition. He struggled to put a brave face on his condition
but was clearly drained of all his strength. I instructed Stachys to do nothing else but care for Simon.

By noon, we had arrived at Antioch, and I immediately dispatched Herminos to search for a Christian household. Simon was in great need of attention, and I imagined that fellowship with other Christians might assist him in his recovery. Herminos returned to the ship an hour later and led us to the house of Leochares, a Christian householder. Leochares has a guest wing attached to his house and was pleased to let us impose on him, especially since Simon is a Christian brother.

We have now been in residence here for two days, and I felt compelled to write to inform you of our troubles. Perhaps you could ensure that news of Simon's condition is reported to the Christians who gather in the house of Antonius in Pergamum. They will want to pray for his health. Leochares knows of a ship sailing for Ephesus in two days' time, and I have instructed Herminos to do whatever he can to establish a contact on the ship who will deliver this letter to you.

I will write again soon, if possible. For now, my concern is for Simon alone, and I pray to his god, hoping that he will look graciously upon us all.

ANTIPAS' SECOND ANTIOCH LETTER

Antipas, traveling nobleman;

To Luke and Calpurnius, friends and Ephesian men of note;

Greetings.

After hearing of a ship scheduled to sail for Ephesus later this week, I decided to inform you of recent events, with the hopes that Herminos can again persuade a willing passenger to deliver this to you.

I continue to reside in the house of Leochares, a Christian benefactor of the city of Antioch. Simon remains in residence here, although he has shown no sign of improvement from his critical condition. I have given Herminos and Stachys the responsibility of caring for his needs, and Leochares' household doctor has done much to relieve his suffering, but their combined efforts have had little effect in staving off the illness from which he suffers. I fear for his life but can do nothing more to help him. I will not resume my travels to Caesarea until his condition is determined one way or another, for better or for worse.

In the meantime, I have spent my many free hours investigating the city of Syrian Antioch and its history. I have learned much from my discussions with others in the courtyards of local temples and have discovered a new appreciation for the historic importance of this city. It has been a significant political and cultural center for generations, largely because of its strategic location on the crossroads of travel routes by both land and sea. Its magnificent architecture is bettered only by Rome and Alexandria, and its population is huge, with estimates above half a million people, including a large Jewish population. The traditional Jewish religion continues to have a high and respected profile here, with a significant number of local non-Jews converting to its way of life or at least honoring the god of the Jews.

But it is the importance of this city in the rise of the Christian movement that has impressed me. I was especially interested to note that our host, Leochares, is the grandson of a man named Manaen, a childhood friend of Herod Antipas and one who later became a follower of Christ and relocated to Antioch [Acts 13:1]. Manaen was one of the early leaders of an Antiochene Christian community that, along with other Antiochene Christian communities, was among the first to welcome Jewish and non-Jewish members into its fellowship. Consequently, these Christians were also among the first to implement guidelines to enable and promote mutuality between Jewish and gentile members at Christian gatherings. The problem of different ethnic groups living in harmony with one another is as old as the ages and probably has shaped the course of human history more than any other factor. But the Antiochene Christians, along with other Christians in Jerusalem and elsewhere, take radical steps to ensure that Christians of all different groups and races can unite in their common worship of Jesus and in their mutual support of one another, while still respecting one another's differences. They associate their efforts in this with Jesus' own life and teaching, in which boundaries among different groups of people were managed in new ways as the empire of God emerged through him.

As a guest of Leochares, I have attended one gathering of Christians at the house of a well-educated young man, Ignatius, and have found many similarities with the gathering of those in the house of Antonius at Pergamum. Both are concerned for the care of the poor and needy, and both are intent on worshiping only Jesus Christ as the sovereign lord. But there are also significant differences between these two groups of Christians. The group that gathers in the house of Ignatius is finding it necessary to form a clearly defined leadership structure. A point of discussion at the gathering I attended was whether tiered leadership roles should be created within the gathering, in association with other Christian groups. Many seemed to favor a three-tiered structure, distinguishing among what they called deacons, presbyters, and a bishop. These discussions were precipitated by the sentiment that dangerous theories had become rife in the Antiochene region and had too easily attached themselves to Christian tradition. An organized structure of leadership and authority was seen as one means of preventing the increase of heretical views and of preserving the Christian tradition. All this is a world away from the simple gathering of Christians at Pergamum, where problems of this kind are not as discernible, and more elementary matters are pressing.

While attending the gathering at Ignatius' house, I learned of another manuscript that recounts the life of Jesus of Nazareth, said to have been written by a man named Matthew, a member of a neighboring group of Christians here in Antioch. A copy of the manuscript is kept at Ignatius' house. Just as I have read sections of your monograph for the Christians gathered at Antonius' house, so the Christians at Ignatius' house read sections of Matthew's account at their gatherings. I quickly read a few sections of it and was intrigued by its similarities to your own monograph, as well as its differences. When I mentioned, Luke, that I had studied your monograph, Ignatius kindly suggested that I take Matthew's and study it during the week. (He also looked forward to adding a copy of your monograph to his library in due course.) I have not been able to study Matthew's work thoroughly, of course, since I have had access to it for only a few days. I have read it through once, however, and have benefited from its portrait of Jesus, the wise Jewish rabbi and the incarnation of the Jewish god who abides with his people. One passage in particular has become a partner to me each day. I first read it to Simon three days ago as he lay in his bed suffering from a heavy fever, and since then every day he has asked for it to be read to him two or three times. It reads like this:

> When the Son of Man comes in his glory, and all the angels with him, he will sit on his throne in heavenly glory. All the nations will be gathered before him, and he will separate the people one from another as a shepherd separates the sheep from the goats. He will put the sheep on his right and the goats on his left.
>
> Then the King will say to those on his right, "Come, you who are blessed by my father; take your inheritance, the kingdom prepared for you since the creation of the world. For I was hungry and you gave me something to eat. I was thirsty and you gave me something to drink. I was a stranger and you gave me hospitality. I needed clothes and you clothed me. I was sick and you looked after me. I was in prison and you came to visit me."
>
> Then the righteous will answer him, "Lord, when did we see you hungry and feed you, or thirsty and give you something to drink? When did we see you a stranger and give you hospitality, or needing clothes and clothe you? When did we see you sick or in prison and go to visit you?"
>
> The King will reply, "I tell you the truth, whatever you did for one of the least of these brothers of mine, you did for me." [Matt. 25:31–40]

These have become words of comfort to Simon, I believe, who disadvantaged himself by caring for the young woman Galatia and her suffering baby in their time of need on board the *Isis*. Simon hears them as words of promise: If the father of Jesus Christ sees fit not to save him from his fever, Simon will nonetheless be restored to wholeness in the glory of the empire of Israel's god, vindicated by Jesus Christ, the exalted Son of Man, who knows the plight of the suffering and looks kindly upon those who suffer for them. Although he may never again see his own children, Simon prays that someone near them might care for them, just as he cared for the needs of the child of another. "There would be no more needy people," he whispered to me yesterday, "if the empire of the gracious god caught hold in the hearts of everyone."

I will send word again, as necessary.

Antipas' Caesarean Letter

Antipas, nobleman of Caesarea;

To Luke and the noble Calpurnius;

Greetings.

I write to you from Caesarea, where I have returned after an absence of nearly a year. I have been here for three weeks now, reunited with my friends and family. But what should have been a joyous reunion has been tinged with sadness, since Simon ben Joseph, my traveling companion and friend, did not accompany me here. He died nearly a month ago in Antioch, overcome in his struggle for life by an unrelenting fever. He had no final words of note but died peacefully in his sleep during the night. Leochares arranged for Simon to be buried alongside other Christian Jews at Antioch. And so the life of a brave soul ended there. Simon was indeed a man of honor, and I will speak only well of him for as long as I live.

After Simon's death, I arranged for passage on the next ship bound for Caesarea, and within a few days I arrived in Caesarea in the heat of the summer sun. Androneikos, my son who now has charge over all the businesses and the household, was pleased to welcome me home at last. (While in Antioch I had sent word to him about my delay.) The following day he held a grand banquet to welcome me, so I was quickly surrounded by old friends and colleagues whom I sorely missed while in Pergamum. I am glad to report that Androneikos continues to prosper as the businesses thrive, and his oversight of the household is impeccable.

Early on in my time here I sent Stachys and Herminos into Galilee to see if they could discover anything about Simon's family. They first went to one of our family vineyards to the northwest of Tiberias to confer with the manager, who had dealings with Simon several years ago. He had overseen the termination of Simon's tenancy on the land when Simon had no longer been able to pay what was required of him, so of course the manager remembered him. He offered a few vague leads as to the possible whereabouts of Simon's six children, but Stachys and Herminos were unable to locate any of them. It seems they have dispersed or become slaves; possibly some are dead. Fortunately, Stachys and Herminos were able to locate Simon's widow, Mary. She had been taken in by one of her brothers and his wife, a childless couple who operate a small merchant trade out of Sepphoris. My servants gave her the news of Simon's death and related to her all that had happened to him in his efforts to provide for his family. She bore her sadness bravely, admitting that she never imagined that Simon would return. He had been frail for much of his later life, and she foresaw as little future for him in Pergamum as there had been for him in Galilee. Stachys and Herminos stayed with her a few hours and then departed to return to me, leaving for Mary two gold rings and one silver goblet. I had instructed my servants to use these to improve the lot of any of Simon's relatives they happened to find. Mary was grateful, thinking that she might use the proceeds of their sale to continue the search for her children.

For my part, I have remained in Caesarea since arriving from Antioch. I had imagined traveling to Tyre to see former business associates there, but the summer heat is unmerciful, and the prospect of travel of any kind is now unattractive. The idea of visiting the city of Jerusalem, as Calpurnius had done, has also fallen victim to the heat, especially since Calpurnius' visit to the city was marked by disappointment at its desperate condition after being humiliated by Roman forces two decades ago. Moreover, I have heard reports that a good number of leading Jews have relocated in the city of Jamnia, just south of here, to the west of Jerusalem. There they are seeking to reconceptualize the Jewish way of life now that the temple of Israel's god has been destroyed. Evidently, a leading view among them is that, without recourse to the temple, atonement for sin is made as they repent of their wrongdoing, worship their god, pray to him, and serve him in heartfelt acts of kindness. I have heard that a dispute continues among them concerning the legitimacy of Rome's overlordship of Judea. Some are still disgruntled by that state of affairs, while others are resigned to it.

I intend to begin my return journey to Pergamum in a week's time. I will inquire as to whether any ships are traveling to Smyrna or Ephesus. If I find only a vessel bound for Smyrna, I will of course take passage on that, then travel from Smyrna to Pergamum by land. If a vessel is traveling directly to Ephesus, however, I will gladly seek passage on it, with the hopes of seeing you briefly before returning to Pergamum.

In the meantime, I have several more banquets to attend here in Caesarea. I do enjoy these occasions of fun and frivolity, but they mean something different to me now than they did in the past. Previously, I would have been the first to use them as opportunities to parade my honor, intent on maintaining and enhancing my prospects. Having removed myself from the cut and thrust of Caesarean life, it is easier now not to take those dynamics too seriously. But doing so makes them seem somewhat hollow and lacking of substance. I am as good as any man at flagrantly displaying my opulence, ensuring that I am seen with other notable civic leaders and generally promoting myself. But these seem to be things of little purpose in the grand scheme of things. I am searching to find an explanation for my recently acquired dissatisfaction with a way of life that has been ingrained in me throughout the course of my long life. That explanation must have something to do with my experiences since leaving Caesarea. In the past few months, I have been exposed to the desperate needs of others and have begun to view them with a sympathetic eye. As a consequence, the single-minded purpose of the gala events of the elite here at Caesarea seems almost woeful, pitiful perhaps, involving little else than self-interest. Any single banquet that I have attended in the past few weeks would have provided well over two years' worth of meals for Galatia and her little baby. Could it be that the code of honor I have attempted to preserve my entire life is simply a self-perpetuating form of societal machinations that has the potential to inflict harm? And if so, might the code of honor itself have shameful side effects? You can see that, although I am not pondering the great works of Homer or of Luke, I remain a seeker of truth.

I am contemplating resigning my position as overseer of the renovation of the Pergamene Asklepion. There are plenty of young upstarts who would be keen to pick up where I left off, and I am content to let the honor fall to one of them. I no longer have the heart to invest myself in this project when I could be investing my diminishing energies in other things of value. Perhaps my return to Pergamum will cause me to change my mind on this, but at this time my interest in bolstering an important pillar of Pergamene life has waned.

Perhaps I will see you again in Ephesus if I gain passage on a ship. If not, I will write to you from Pergamum when time permits. Until I see you again, may you be blessed by the high god of goodness.[1]

1. Dates pertaining to letter collection 12 are likely to be as follows: On 15 June, Antipas left Pergamum, arriving in Ephesus on 18 June, where he stayed for three days. Departing by ship on 22 June, he sailed for four days before arriving in Antioch on 25 June. He stayed in Antioch for two weeks until 2 July. During this time he wrote his two Antiochene letters. He departed for Caesarea on 3 July, arriving on 6 July. He wrote his Caesarean letter on 27 July.

MAY HIS WILL BE DONE

Antipas' Letter

Antipas, citizen of Rome, lover of all things good and beneficial, and seeker for truth;

To my friends Luke, lover of god, and Calpurnius, preeminent citizen of Ephesus;

Grace be with you.

I have now returned to Pergamum, having been refreshed in my travels by your mutual kindness. Your hospitality to me and my entourage on the way was most welcome, especially since the effects of time's passage have apparently worsened my abilities to travel. Nonetheless, we have returned to Pergamum without further complication [allusion uncertain], welcomed back by the kindly Euphemos, who, true to his word, reserved my rooms in his house in my absence.

I have returned with some unease, however. Your worry about the situation in Pergamum was well-founded. The first disturbing indicator came when, on my first night back, Euphemos gently suggested that I sever my connections with the Christians who assemble in the house of Antonius. Although this was presented as a suggestion to preserve my own good name, I was certain that Euphemos was concerned to protect his own at the same time. It became clear that, if I continued to be associated with those particular Christians while living in Euphemos' house, I might compromise his own standing within the city. It seems that the Christians who gather at Antonius' house are suspected of antisocial behavior, as those who compromise the city of Pergamum in the eyes of Rome. This reputation has come about, it seems, solely through the actions of Demetrius, that well-meaning stonemason, husband to Diotis and caretaker of darling Nouna. Although he has continually worked hard to pro-

163

mote the good, his feisty petulance has put him in the center of the city's recent gaze. I was devastated to learn that Demetrius is now being held in custody by the city magistrates.

After hearing this from Euphemos, I went early the next day to Antonius' house, expecting to hear of these recent events from him and Mania, after which I would need to evaluate my own situation. It should not have come as a surprise to find that Antonius had taken Diotis and Nouna into his own household to provide for their security. The charges against Demetrius were substantial enough to suggest that retribution against his family might follow, and Antonius took action to prevent that from happening. This act alone could endanger Antonius' standing within the city. Although he is clearly aware of this danger, it seems not to have factored into his attitude toward Diotis and Nouna.

I am now able to reconstruct the events leading up to this present situation, of which I know you will want to be informed. It seems that this crisis was precipitated by a disagreement between Demetrius and the managers of the Pergamene stonemasons' guild, the strongest guild of the city and one fiercely loyal to the emperor. Demetrius' membership within the guild had become progressively strained as he began to make vocal protestation against some of the guild's practices, especially its unrestrained honoring of the emperor. There had been a recent upsurge in the guild's commitment to display honor for Domitian and to worship him. Demetrius' protests had increased to match the guild's augmented interest in the imperial cult. He had objected in particular to the guild's special banquets held in the emperor's honor, at which incense is burned on the emperor's behalf, sacrifices are offered before images of the emperor and the established gods of Pergamum, and some of the sacrificial meat is eaten in the banquet setting. Demetrius' vocal infractions of civic etiquette brought upon him the ire of the guild. Its managers attempted to discipline him, but without avail. On one occasion, for instance, he was instructed to offer his own sacrifice to Domitian upon the Great Altar of the gods in the acropolis, but the deadline for that action lapsed without his compliance.

At this point, he probably would simply have been ejected from the guild, falling among the vulnerable ranks of the unemployed. Unfortunately, things took a different course once Demetrius' vocal denunciations caught the attention of civic authorities. They took notice of Demetrius' public portrayal of Domitian as the ambassador of evil who usurps the universal authority of the true god. Along with this, Demetrius had regularly indicted the imperial cult that has rooted itself firmly in Pergamum.

Taken into custody to stand trial before the civic officials, Demetrius refused to retract his subversive claims and consistently declared Jesus Christ to be the sole ruler of the universe. The officials castigated him as an atheist [one who opposes traditional Roman religion] and an antisocial miscreant. His open attacks on the pillars of civic life were deemed antagonistic to the well-being of the city and dangerous to society in general. Sentenced to death, he is in prison awaiting the next gladiatorial event, now less than two weeks away, to be attended by the emperor himself. At those games, under the emperor's own gaze, Demetrius is scheduled to be executed as a criminal against the state, an example to deter others of a similar ilk. Only two courses of action will save Demetrius of that fate. First, he could recant his charges against the emperor, offer sacrifices before the emperor's image, and eat the meat of altar sacrifices. Second, on the day of the games themselves, the emperor might take the occasion to show leniency, demonstrating before the crowds the extent of his graciousness and goodness. No one knows what might happen.

Meanwhile, it seems that little Nouna has been traumatized by this series of events. She refuses to speak, is not eating much, and keeps herself secluded. The joy of life that shone from her eyes and delighted me so much prior to my journey is now nowhere to be seen. Diotis is naturally distraught, her tears continually streaming down her face.

I mentioned none of this to Demetrius when I gained access to his prison cell later in the day. He too showed signs of stress. He has lost a significant amount of weight, and his back shows evidence of scourging. His cell is dark, musty, and foul in smell. But he remains alert in mind, determined in spirit, and confident in his singular faith in Jesus Christ. Evidently, Kalandion had already visited him several days earlier in the hope of deterring him from his persistent atheism. Kalandion, who is clearly concerned about his own reputation as a Christ worshiper, suggested that allegiance to Jesus Christ is not incompatible with worship of the Roman emperor and the lesser gods. Moreover, eating meat sacrificed to idols is not a religious offense. According to Kalandion, because all food comes from the most high god, and because idols have no real existence or power, Christians should not worry about eating sacrificial food. Demetrius thought that, in principle, Kalandion's argument about idol meat was correct. However, he felt that eating meat sacrificed to idols in the context of a guild banquet would signal his compliance with the imperial cult and would involve a compromise in his singular devotion to Jesus Christ. That was a step he was unprepared to make. Kalandion departed from Demetrius' prison cell unsuccessful in his attempts to find an acceptable compromise.

In our conversation, Demetrius spoke about his decision to take a stand against the increasing local pressures to conform to imperialistic propaganda and the cult of emperor worship. He feels that the emperor's claims to divinity, perpetuated by the local imperial priesthood, are simply the most obscene and despicable demonstration of human self-aggrandizement. It is this characteristic that he thinks is deeply embedded within the empire, eating away at its heart as a cancer devours its host. Demetrius recounted how the story of Jesus' life, death, and resurrection helped him to see Rome for what it really is. Unmasked, it is little more than a peddler of human pride and self-centeredness under the guise of divine legitimization. The human traits of conceit and self-importance propelled Rome to world supremacy, and now those traits are conspiring to worship themselves in the embodied form of the emperor. Demetrius said that he wanted no part of this narcissistic paganism, preferring to give his allegiance instead to the empire of god that Jesus had spoken of, practiced, and embodied.

Demetrius feels that the Christians who gather at Antonius' house have caught momentary glimpses of that empire in their corporate gatherings. He claims that the invigoration of those moments surpasses anything he has ever experienced. To eat together without being bound by societal expectations; to learn, study, and worship together as a group of people, males and females, from a variety of races and locations, each with different roles in society and different levels of civic status and economic power—these corporate occasions are, for Demetrius, embodiments of the divine empire proclaimed and inaugurated by Jesus. These unprecedented phenomena are not the product of a local deity or tribal god. They emerge as the manifestation of the power of the ultimate god, the universal god, the god of all people, the god responsible for the creation of life. This god alone has the power to defeat the forces of chaos, evil, and death. So it is not surprising that Jesus was raised from the dead, signaling the overthrow of those forces by the most high god. Only he has such authority and power, not Rome. As a result of Rome's claim to prevail over these forces of chaos, some good is being done in the name of stability, but that good only serves to cloak the way in which the chaotic forces of self-interest and conceit permeate the Roman empire. In Demetrius' view, Jesus' life challenged those forces; his death absorbed them; and his resurrection defeated them. These events have set in motion the power of god's spirit to inspire new patterns of living in those loyal to Jesus. In those patterns of life lie the testimony that the most high god is sovereign over the forces of evil and chaos. It is against this backdrop, Demetrius told me, that he views his impending death. Despite its ghastly prospect, he is willing to remain faithful to his god, who in turn will be faithful to him, restoring him to life in the final resurrection of which Jesus spoke.

It was pointless to try to dissuade him from his intended course of action, and I was unsure of what to say as I left him, other than to compliment his bravery. As I rose to leave, Demetrius rose too and prayed to the god of Israel on behalf of both of us, seeking wisdom, courage, and faithfulness.

After leaving Demetrius' prison cell, I returned late at night to my rooms in Euphemos' house, which I then vacated the next morning. Euphemos and I did not exchange much conversation that morning, for we both knew the implications of my departure. I requested that he pass on to the other city officials my resignation from the post of overseeing the renovation of the Asklepion, and he agreed to do so, expressing his regrets. I then donated my servants to Euphemos' service in exchange for his kindness over the past months and took with me only Stachys and Glykeros, my scribe.

I dictate this letter to you from Attaea, one day's travel from Pergamum, where I have taken residence in a humble inn near the Aegean Sea. I am not known here and, having connections with neither the house of Antonius nor the house of Euphemos, I can consider these matters dispassionately. I am not sure whether I will ever again return to Pergamum.

I hope to write to you soon, good friend. You remain a faithful guide in my journey for truth. I would ask that you join me in praying to the father of Jesus Christ with regard to these matters. May his will be done.

Farewell.

LUKE'S LETTER

To Antipas, seeker of truth and promoter of the good;

From Luke, your faithful friend and follower of Jesus Christ;

Grace be with you.

Your report on recent events in Pergamum has greatly troubled us, and I together with Calpurnius and others who worship with us continue to pray for all those who are caught up in these events. We have prayed that God's Spirit will move in your heart and enlighten your thoughts so that you might know the course he would have you follow in this time of testing. Although your last letter identified me as a faithful guide in your search for truth, I fear I can offer no words for your guidance other than my prayers for you to the most high God. You have read my volume on Jesus' life, death, and resurrection, having studied it and its implications more closely than many. You are more aware of what is at stake than most. You have come to know the Christians of Antonius' house. With them you have worshiped, eaten, studied, served others, laughed, and grieved. Some of them you have taken to your heart as if they were your own family. Now it seems you are being forced to decide whether you will stand alongside them in a dark hour. That decision, dear friend, is a matter for you only. I know your mind to be clear, your wisdom to be noble, and your heart to be generous. I will continue to support you in friendship no matter what decision you act upon.

You are not alone in these troubled times, dear Antipas. I have recently heard unfortunate news about a Christian prophet who has paid a heavy penalty for giving voice to views deemed unacceptable by the local leaders of the imperial cult here in Ephesus. This man, whose name is John, was recently deported by the local Ephesian authorities in an effort to stifle his testimony that the one who sits upon the eternal and sovereign throne is not the emperor but Jesus Christ, whom we Christians proclaim as Lord. Although an elderly man, this John is now in exile, subjected to house arrest on the nearby island of Patmos [Rev. 1:9]. In this manner he has been silenced and made an example.

I fear these are dark days for many of us, but we are not the first to experience testing of this sort. In the second volume of my historical monograph, I mention others who met similar fates, including Stephen, martyred for his faith in Jerusalem, and James, a disciple of Jesus who was beheaded by the tetrarch Herod Agrippa I [42 c.e.]. The great apostles Paul and Peter met similar ends, although I did not record those matters in that second volume. I have instructed my scribe to begin a new copy of that volume, which I will happily send to you once it is finished, as we have already agreed.

In the meantime, virtuous Antipas, continue to consider the faithfulness of Jesus Christ, and may his Spirit live in your heart and life. You are in our prayers at all times. May the grace of the Lord Jesus Christ be with you, to the eternal glory of the most high God.[1]

1. The events for this letter collection are likely to be dated as follows: Antipas left Caesarea on 13 August, arriving in Ephesus on 26 or 27 August (traveling against the prevailing winds). After staying one night at the house of Calpurnius, he left for Pergamum on 27 or 28 August, arriving in Pergamum on 31 August. He met with Demetrius and others on 1 September and moved to Attaea on 2 September, writing to Luke on 4 September. Stachys left Attaea with Antipas' letter on the morning of 5 September, arriving in Pergamum in the late afternoon of 8 September. If Luke replied immediately (and his letter is short enough for that), Stachys would have left Pergamum on 9 September, arriving in Attaea on 12 September. The Pergamene gladiatorial games were scheduled to be held on 15 September.

THE POSSESSIONS
OF OUR COMMON
CREATOR

ANTONIUS' LETTER

Antonius, nobleman of Pergamum;

To Luke in the house of Calpurnius, a brother in the Lord;

Grace be to you in the name of our Lord Jesus Christ.

I am writing to you on the calends of Domitianus [1 October] to alert you to the recent events that have overtaken us here in Pergamum, which you may have heard of already by informal report. Knowing of Antipas' affection and respect for you, I have taken it upon myself to send you a personal report. Our beloved Antipas, citizen, nobleman, benefactor, and friend, has given up his life to the most high God. Mania and I have been distraught by this and its implications, and I write as much to inform you as to ask for your prayers and encouragement in these desperate times.

The night before his death, Antipas came to my house after the sun had set and requested that I provide safekeeping for the scribal copies of his correspondence with you. He also deposited with me other documents that I have since examined, finding them to comprise official records, personal reports, and business inventories. I see from the copy of his last letter to you that you have been fully informed of the situation surrounding Demetrius' arrest. Antipas also informed you of his own departure from Pergamum and retreat to Attaea on the coast, where he resided for a week and a half. He returned to Pergamum the night before the Pergamene gladiatorial contests several weeks ago, and on that same night he appeared at my house with his documentation.

On that night, Antipas and I had a brief conversation about Demetrius' situation. I could see that he was tremendously uncomfortable discussing the matter, and his face appeared to be shadowy gray. Knowing that he was no longer resident in Euphemos' house, I suggested that he consider my house to be his own for as long as it proved beneficial to him, but he refused, despite my protests. He asked only two things: to see Nouna briefly and to leave his servants Stachys and Glykeros with me. I agreed and took him to Nouna's bedside, where he stroked her hair as she slept quietly. In the darkness, I remember thinking how his aged hands appeared to be both soft and strong in this gentle touch.

Diotis, the girl's mother, woke to find him there and called his name. When he responded, Antipas' voice had the same softness and strength that was in his touch. "Have no fear. All will be well," he said. Then he kissed Nouna's forehead lovingly, covered her with a blanket, and withdrew from the house. He stopped at the door and mumbled something about wanting to offer Stachys his freedom after his final trip from Pergamum to Ephesus in the near future (a comment I did not understand until later). After thanking me for my kindness, he embraced me and departed alone into the night.

I saw him next in the amphitheater the following day, the day of the Pergamene gladiatorial games [15 September]. The amphitheater was filled to capacity, with an even larger number of noblemen in attendance for this event than for the first event six months ago. I sat in the *tribunal editoris* [the area designated for highly regarded civic magistrates alongside the holder of the games] with other magistrates. Rufinus, the host, and Kalandion, his assistant in the organization of the games, were seated in pride of place. The emperor and his party sat directly across the arena in the imperial podium. Although Rufinus was the host of the games, the emperor obviously received the most attention. His entourage included a host of nobleman and advisors and his cousin Flavius Clemens. Although the emperor drew the gaze of the crowd, Rufinus' own reputation as host of the games was bolstered by the emperor's presence.

I was not an enthusiastic spectator at the games, not least since my heart was downtrodden with sorrow, knowing that Demetrius, our friend and brother in the Lord, was scheduled to meet a horrendous death in the course of the day. Although I could do nothing to change the outcome, I thought it best to attend, for the sake of both Demetrius and Diotis. Upon my urging, Diotis had decided not to attend the games but to remain in my house, knowing that her own heart would be torn to pieces were she to watch Demetrius meet his death in the jaws of wild animals. But she requested that I attend the games to confirm Demetrius' bravery and courage in my own testimony. We also thought that perhaps

I could catch Demetrius' eye long enough to offer him a brotherly embrace prior to his ordeal. And so, with a heavy heart, I attended the games.

The day commenced along the normal lines, with the parade and the beast hunts taking up most of the morning. At lunchtime, the execution of criminals began. Demetrius' execution was to take place after the execution of the freemen by the sword; the crimes with which he had been charged were considered heinous enough to be worthy of death by animal mauling. After twenty or so other freemen were executed, Demetrius was brought into the arena, in chains, accompanied by a handler and a leading civic official. He was taken to stand before the emperor's box, where the emperor and his entourage were seated. Although frail in physical appearance, Demetrius carried himself with boldness and conviction. The emperor motioned for silence and then signaled the official to speak. Over the bestial noises protruding from the animal complex, he stated the charges against Demetrius: blasphemy against the emperor, criminal treason against the state, and atheism.

The emperor, probably having been informed of the case prior to the day, asked for no clarification of the charges. Instead, he announced his wish to hear what the host of the games thought of the case against this Christian. Rufinus, almost on cue, stood in the *tribunal editoris* and announced to the emperor that he had personally studied some of the life of Jesus Christ. From his study, Rufinus had concluded that the teachings of Jesus Christ were a Jewish superstition that posed something of a political danger to the empire because those of weaker minds might perceive such teachings as a challenge to the legitimacy of the eternal city of Rome. Nonetheless, he also pointed out that many Pergamenes who worship Jesus Christ do not compromise their imperial loyalty or their worship of the traditional gods. As an example, he mentioned Kalandion, who had acted as his personal assistant in organizing these games. (At this, Kalandion took the occasion to draw the emperor's gaze to himself by rising from his seat and bowing in the direction of the imperial box.) Rufinus pointed out further that some Christians associated with Demetrius are also noblemen of Pergamum and have not committed treasonable offenses. (I imagined he was referring to me and to Antipas, but I shared no exchange of glance with Rufinus.) Rufinus was led to believe, he announced, that Demetrius stood accused of offenses that were applicable to him alone and no one else. But the charges were legitimate and were to be met with execution, lest others join in his treason. Rufinus then bowed and seated himself.

The crowd continued its silence, which was broken only by the words of the emperor. He announced that, in contrast to common supposition, his general inclination is to be generous and merciful to all his subjects but that, since a local nobleman had made a specific request, he would permit the request. He instructed that Demetrius be prepared for execution by animal slaughter and pronounced a blessing on Demetrius' soul. At this, the crowd erupted in shouts of approval, which were accepted as a compliment by the emperor. This interaction between the emperor and Rufinus had probably been devised prior to the games. The staging had proceeded as planned, and the emperor emerged with his reputation enhanced and with Roman justice intact.

What did not proceed as planned happened next. As Demetrius was being removed from the arena to prepare him for the slaughter, a solitary figure emerged from somewhere, walking directly toward the imperial podium. It was Antipas, dressed in attire that clearly attested to his stature as a member of the elite, but walking with the gait of a burdened man. As he neared the emperor, the imperial guards rushed him and tried to sweep him back, but the emperor's interest had been aroused by this unprecedented sight, and he instructed his guards simply to hold the man. Standing where Demetrius had just stood, Antipas' initial words were lost under the noise of the crowd, whereupon a hush came over the amphitheater. The emperor asked his name and purpose. I will attempt to do justice to Antipas' forthright words.

I, most excellent Domitian, am Antipas, a nobleman of your empire, the recipient of divine favor in my birth and business. The city of Tyre was my base for accruing great profit from my landholdings in Galilee, and the city of Caesarea Maritima has been my home for many years. My name is taken from the son of Herod the Great, Herod Antipas, a great tetrarch of Galilee and promoter of Rome. I have only recently come to Pergamum, the citadel of the gods, to spend my final years in quiet contemplation, to worship the gods in a city loyal to the emperor, and to benefit from the healing effects of Asklepios as my bones become arthritic.

Throughout my years, like my father and his father, I have never ceased to work for the common good of the empire. I have been one to acquire many possessions through my diligence and to spend my wealth freely through generosity. I have supported the populace in times of famine. I have provided baths, statues, fountains, pavements, and spectacles for the cities and have sought to surpass my peers in doing good. I am no rogue and have no passion for sedition. In my short time in this region, I have already acted as benefactor to the cities of Pergamum, Ephesus, and Miletus. Indeed, the statue of you, our powerful emperor, that stands at the entrance to this city came into being exclusively through my benefaction. I, along with the honorable Kalandion, assisted our great nobleman Rufinus in organizing the gladiatorial games held earlier this year in your honor. So the words that I speak are not those of a scoundrel but of one who all his life has been loyal to you and the great emperors of Rome before you.

The man who has just appeared before you is Demetrius, someone I have known for a short period of time. Although he is an artisan, I have found him to be a man of great insight and wisdom. I have shared a common bond of association with him for several months, gathering with him and others to eat, study, worship, and serve others in the name of Jesus Christ. In these gatherings, I have seen the start of something that has refreshed my soul, tired as it was from years of striving to promote my own reputation and honor. These gatherings testify to a new form of society, a truly generous society, wherein honor is not zealously reserved for the few who can manipulate it for their own benefit but is recognized as a quality of all people. No one is more surprised than I am to find that what motivates me now is not a commitment to the Pax Romana [the peace brought about by Rome] but a commitment to the empire of the God of Israel. That God is, I now believe, the eternal, sovereign, and blessed Lord of all, the creator God whose mercy knows no boundaries. I also must affirm, consequently, that Rome's authority is legitimate as long as it does not transgress the boundaries of the empire of God in which Jesus is Lord.

These words are not themselves seditious. Should you hear them as such, I would appeal to your merciful character, which you have today advertised. I would plead with you, then, to release Demetrius, by your grace. Should Rome's justice require a victim, then let that victim be me. I will take his punishment. After all, I have acted as a sponsor to Demetrius and his family for several months now, just as a patron sponsors a client. If a footman is knocked down and killed by a chariot, it is not the chariot but the chariot driver who is culpable. If a ship smashes into the rocks, it is the sailor at the tiller who takes the blame. So too, if you deem Demetrius to have committed an offense, I, as his sponsor, must take the responsibility. You may consider me an irresponsible nobleman who has permitted scandal to rise up under his own nose unaware. My death will serve as an example to others, and you will be shown to be both merciful and unswerving. In your wisdom, let your mercy fall upon Demetrius and your justice fall upon me, great Domitian.

The silence continued to pervade the amphitheater, and for moments the emperor said nothing. Finally, he pronounced, "Let it be as you have said. Free Demetrius with a caution, and may he think on the emperor's kindness. Prepare Antipas for the slaughter as if he were a common criminal. And may all others know of the emperor's intrinsic clemency and unmovable justice." Antipas answered with the following: "You and I are the possessions of our common Creator, and we both are enslaved to his will. You have done your part; now I must do mine. I do so without fear, complaint, or regret, looking forward to the glorious return of the Son of Man, my Lord, my God, and my Savior, whose kingdom is eternal. May the God and father of Jesus Christ preserve my soul and bless my brothers and sisters in the Lord."

The amphitheater filled with the sound of the spectators discussing this unprecedented spectacle. Without showing any emotion, Antipas was taken and prepared for slaughter. Demetrius, who knew only of Antipas' entry into the arena, was simply told that his life had been spared. He was beaten and then ejected from the amphitheater complex, unaware of the conditions of his release.

After a few minutes, Antipas emerged, stripped of his garments except for a simple tunic and bound with chains. Escorted by four guards, he was led to a place near the *tribunal editoris*. Fires had already been prepared around the amphitheater to facilitate the execution of some of the criminals. Antipas was led to the small fire nearest to the *tribunal editoris* and was made to face the emperor. His face was pale, but he held himself with dignity. Then the slaughtered carcass of a magnificent bull was carried in and laid before him. Two of the arena boys cut open the carcass through the throat, breast, and stomach. Its entrails poured out on to the sand. They cleaned out the carcass and cleared away the innards. The guards placed three chains under the carcass. They then forced Antipas to place himself inside the emptied carcass, folding his legs within its body. The carcass was chained together, fully encompassing Antipas within it. Lifting the carcass with a metal pole, the guards rigged it up so that it stood over the nearby fire whose flames burned low but hot. Downhearted, I could not stay to watch and departed the amphitheater in sorrow. As I departed, Rufinus' eye caught mine. I saw no sorrow for the terrible events that had now befallen his friend Antipas; instead, the look on his face seemed to say that justice had been done. I have learned that no sound was ever heard from Antipas throughout the ordeal, although his death must have been slow and excruciating. He died, as he had lived, with honor, courage, and nobility.

Returning to my house, I was met with some gladness. After his release, Demetrius had painfully made his way straight to my house, knowing that Diotis and Nouna were in residence there. He greeted an astounded Diotis with a joyful embrace. Nouna evidently was bewildered by his return but soon was playing with him as if he had never been gone. The family's joy was tinged with remorse upon hearing of Antipas' bold death. Demetrius continues to be distraught by these events, and his soul bears scars almost as deep as the wounds on his body. Living in prison for some weeks and coming to the brink of death affected him mightily. With Diotis and Nouna, he will continue to stay at my house, recuperating from his ordeal until preparations can be made for his relocation. It is clear that, with his reputation as an antisocial miscreant, he can no longer work in Pergamum unless he publicly compromises his singular devotion to Jesus Christ. It is also clear that, if he continues to renounce the imperial cult publicly, he will be imprisoned again and killed, and Antipas' death will have been in vain. So Pergamum holds no future for him. Perhaps he will soon return to his hometown in Ancyra. But wherever he goes, he is likely to meet the same dilemma, for the cult of the emperor has taken a strong hold throughout the empire.

Pray for us here in Pergamum, dear friend. Since the time of Demetrius' arrest, the number of people who gather at my house to worship Jesus Christ has dwindled to only a handful. We continue to meet, pray, study, and care for one another and for others, but we do so mindful of the ever present threat that hangs over us. Meanwhile, Kalandion and others continue to worship Jesus alongside the traditional gods at the temple to Rome and Augustus, offering sacrifices to Jesus as a powerful god and to the emperor as the Lord of all the empire. Since the gladiatorial games, Kalandion has enjoyed an enhanced reputation, and many more are worshiping with him than had previously been the case. Rufinus, with his eyes on advancement to a position in the Roman senate, no longer has connections of any sort with Christian gatherings.

I have managed to carry out my normal duties relatively unaffected by the recent ordeal. No one is looking to yoke me with Demetrius as a troublemaker; Rufinus' speech to the emperor has ensured that Demetrius' reputation has not yet spread to the rest of us. Nonetheless, it may be only a matter of time before I too am forced to declare publicly my allegiance to Jesus Christ over the emperor and the traditional gods. I am prepared to do this, I believe, but I also see the case for supporting the Christians in my house under a low profile until either this situation passes or the Lord returns. We pray for God's wisdom to guide us in these troublesome times. Meanwhile, we seek to carry on in love and unity, lest the forces of chaos that Antipas died to oppose should have their way within our own corporate life.

I regret that I could not write to you sooner about these things. Neither strength nor time have assisted me in this, since now more than ever I must be seen as one fully immersed in carrying out his civic duties.

I have sent Stachys to deliver this message, after which he will be free, in accordance with Antipas' veiled suggestion to me on the night before his death. If Stachys should wish to return to my household, I would gladly accept him as a freeman in my service for as long as he wishes. Or perhaps the house of Calpurnius has need of his trustworthy and efficient skills.

Brother Luke, I will keep the letters between you and Antipas in a safe place. Diotis has requested that I keep them until such time as they can be read to Nouna to enable her to know more of the man who died so that her adopted father might live.

I hope to see you soon. You are always welcome in our midst.

May the Lord be with you.

EDITOR'S POSTSCRIPT

Readers of this letter corpus may find the following information helpful.

1. Nothing else is known about Luke, Antonius and Mania, or Demetrius, Diotis, and Nouna.

2. The fate of Flavius Clemens, the cousin of Domitian who accompanied the emperor to the Pergamene games, is known. He was married to Domitilla, the emperor's niece. Although Domitian had long viewed Clemens as a trusted advisor, in 95 C.E. Domitian charged him with being an "atheist," having neglected the traditional religions of Rome. Evidence from the catacombs in Rome suggests that Clemens and Domitilla were sympathetic to Christianity, if not Christians themselves. Domitian exiled Domitilla and executed Clemens as an enemy of the empire.

3. By the mid-90s C.E., Domitian was greatly reviled by the Roman senate. He was murdered on 16 September 96 C.E. by a freeman named Stephanus, who had previously been a procurator of Domitilla. Under the pretense of handing the emperor a document, Stephanus attacked and killed Domitian.

4. The history of Pergamene Christianity after these events is sketchy. In the mid-90s C.E., while in exile on the island of Patmos, the author of the Johannine apocalypse directly addressed Christians in Pergamum as well as six other locations in western Asia Minor (Revelation 2–3). According to him, a sizable portion of the Christian community in Pergamum had compromised its faith in collusion with the imperial cult. With them in view, the author wrote the following in veiled fashion, using imagery from the Old Testament: "I have a few things against you: You have people there who hold to the teaching of Balaam, who taught Balak to entice the Israelites to sin by eating food sacrificed to idols and by committing sexual immorality. Like-

wise you also have those who hold to the teaching of the Nicolaitans"
(Rev. 2:14–15).

5. Approximately fifteen years after these words were written, Ignatius
of Antioch (referred to by Antipas in his second letter from Antioch),
having become a bishop in Antioch, mentions the existence of Christian communities in three of the seven locations identified in Revelation 2–3 (Ephesus, Smyrna, and Philadelphia). No mention is made,
however, of Christian communities in Pergamum. A second- or third-
century C.E. text known as *The Martyrdom of Carpus, Papylus, and
Agothonice* (also known as *The Acts of the Pergamene Martyrs*) gives an
account of three martyrs (two men and one woman) who died for
their Christian testimony in Pergamum. Eusebius, a fourth-century
author, preserved a document entitled *The Letter of the Churches of
Lyons and Vienne*, which records a series of martyrdoms in Gaul in
177 C.E. At one point, that document recalls the death of a man, Attalos, whose family origins lay in Pergamum. Condemned for holding
to the Christian faith, Attalos was scheduled to be executed by wild
beasts at the gladiatorial games, where he met his death with honor.

6. In 132–135 C.E., a second Jewish revolt against Rome took place in
Judea, led by Simeon ben Kosiba. It seems to have been precipitated
by efforts of the emperor Hadrian (emperor 117–138 C.E.) to ban cir-
cumcision and to build a new Roman city, Aelia Capitolina, on the
ruins of the previous city of Jerusalem. A valiant effort by the Jewish
revolutionaries did not result in success. Aelia Capitolina was established, and Rome populated it with gentile settlers, erecting a temple
of Jupiter Capitolinus in the place where the Jerusalem temple had
once stood. The Jewish rabbis relocated to Galilee to complete the
work they had begun in Jamnia (also known as Yavneh), reshaping
Judaism to make it more viable in the absence of the Jerusalem temple. Their efforts survive in the compilation of the Mishnah, the Palestinian Talmud, and other works of the rabbinic period.

Appendix A

Maps

Map 1

The Mediterranean World

Map 2

The Judea/Galilee Region

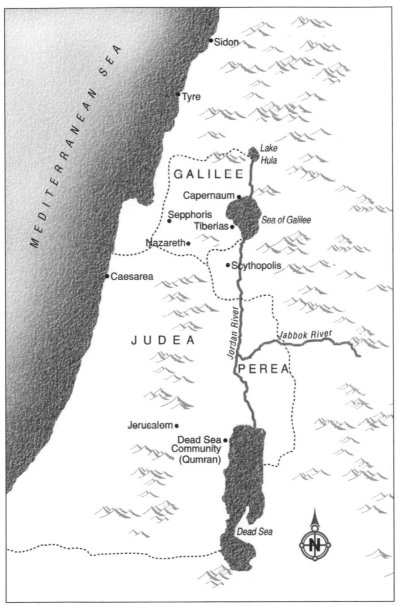

Map 3

Pergamum and Surrounding Area

Appendix B

Characters

Main Characters (in order of appearance)

Brackets contain the number of the letter collection in which the person is first introduced.

Antipas [1]	member of the elite; Roman citizen; owner of Galilean tracts of land; formerly based in Caesarea and Tyre, now based in Pergamum at the house of Euphemos
Calpurnius [1]	son of Theophilus; head of an Ephesian household; host to Luke
Rufinus [1]	member of the elite; Roman citizen; high-ranking official of Pergamum; sponsor of the Pergamene gladiatorial games of 92 C.E.; quickly rising in civic prominence throughout the course of this correspondence
Stachys [1]	one of Antipas' servants and the primary vehicle for delivering correspondence between Pergamum and Ephesus
Luke [2]	author of the canonical Gospel of Luke and the canonical Acts of the Apostles; now based in Ephesus in the house of Calpurnius
Antonius [2]	head of a Pergamene household whose house is used as a base for one Christian group in Pergamum
Kalandion [6]	head of a Pergamene household whose house is used as a base for one Christian group in Pergamum
Simon ben Joseph [8]	former employee of Antipas; nurtured to health by Antonius and part of his household
Demetrius [9]	a stonemason from Ancyra, now based in Pergamum

187

Minor Characters (in order of appearance)

Theophilus [1]	the one to whom Luke wrote his two-volume monograph (the Gospel of Luke, the Acts of the Apostles; cf. Luke 1:3 and Acts 1:1); a bibliophile who had collected numerous volumes of literary treasures; deceased by the time of this correspondence
Domitian [1]	emperor of the Roman empire 81–96 C.E., who increasingly expected to be worshiped as the earthly incarnation of the high god Zeus/Jupiter
Drusus [1]	father of Rufinus
Euphemos [1]	well-established citizen of Pergamum; host to Antipas
Androneikos [3]	Antipas' son, to whom Antipas has left the family business
Quadratus [3]	an elite citizen of Pergamum, with strong connections to Rome
Lysanius Paullus [4]	appointed regional Asiarch in Miletus
Domnos [4]	a servant of Euphemos
Kuseron [4]	a servant of Antipas
Zosimos [5]	a scribe of Luke
Diodorus [6]	an adulated gladiator at the first Pergamene games
Castor [6]	an adulated gladiator at the first Pergamene games
Photinus [6]	an owner of an Alexandrian troop of gladiators
Earinus [7]	Domitian's "favorite boy"
Lycomedes [7]	member of the elite; Roman citizen; high-ranking official of Pergamum
Mania [8]	wife of Antonius; former priestess in the Sanctuary of Demeter and municipal archoness
Glykeros [9]	a scribe of Antipas
Kyrilos [9]	a servant of Antipas
Theodotos [9]	a Pergamene city official
Tullia Spendousa [9]	a Pergamene city official
Octacilius Pollio [9]	a Roman consul, associated with Rufinus
Claudius Charax [9]	a Roman consul, associated with Rufinus
Kyrilla [9]	a songstress who worships with Christians at Antonius' house
Karpos [9]	an Ancyrean trader who worships with Christians at Antonius' house
Nouna [9]	a young girl abandoned by her family
Diotis [10]	Demetrius' wife
Photion [10]	a Christian associated with those who worship at Antonius' house
Herminos [11]	a personal servant of Antipas
Attikos [11]	a scribe and administrator of Antipas
Galatia [12]	a young woman in passage on the ship *Isis*
Leochares [12]	a Christian benefactor in Antioch
Ignatius [12]	a leader of a Christian group in Antioch
Mary [12]	wife of Simon
Flavius Clemens [14]	a Roman nobleman, cousin of Domitian

Appendix C

Historical
and Fictional Aspects
of the Narrative

Author's Preface

The supposition that the Antipas mentioned in Revelation 2:13 had been named after Herod Antipas, the son of Herod the Great and pro-Roman tetrarch who reigned over Galilee during the time of Jesus' ministry, is not necessarily far-fetched. In the first published volumes of the *Lexicon of Greek Personal Names* (sponsored by the British Academy and carried out by the Faculty of Classics, University of Oxford), the name "Antipas" is shown to have been exceedingly rare. In literary and archaeological remains from the ancient world, the name "Antipas" occurs only three times across a sizable area that includes the Aegean Islands, Cyprus, Cyrenaica, Attica, the Peloponnese, western Greece, Sicily, Magna Graecia, and central Greece. See P. M. Fraser and E. Matthews, eds., *A Lexicon of Greek Personal Names*, vol. 1 (Oxford: Clarendon, 1987); vol. 2 (Oxford: Oxford University Press, 1994); vol. 3a (Oxford: Oxford University Press, 1997); and vol. 3b (Oxford: Clarendon, 2000). The name "Antipas" appears only once in volume 2 and twice in volume 3a.

Editor's Preface

The paragraph pertaining to archaeological interest in Pergamum is an accurate reflection of the recent situation. The description of the discovery of the correspondence is fictional.

Letter Collection 1

The following are wholly fictional: the characters Calpurnius, Euphemos, and Stachys; the Pergamene gladiatorial games of 92 C.E.

The following are speculative: Antipas' identity; Theophilus' geographical base.

While Rufinus' identity is fictional, it is based on a historical person, L. Cuspius Pactumeius Rufinus, a consul and influential citizen of Pergamum who was prominent in the early second century C.E. under the emperor Hadrian, just after the time of this narrative. He was one of three men who oversaw the remodeling of the Pergamene temple of Asklepios, rising to a high office, enjoying a profitable relationship with the emperor, and becoming a Roman senator.

The following can be defended historically: the locations of gladiatorial schools; Domitian's identity.

Letter Collection 2

The following is wholly fictional: the character Antonius.

The following are speculative: Luke's geographical base and situation.

The following can be defended historically: the existence of different versions of Homer edited by Crates and by Aristarchos; the reputation of the Pergamene library; Luke's identity.

The library of Pergamum enjoyed a superior reputation in Antipas' day. Having been established by the Attalid king Eumenes II (197–159 B.C.E.), by the late first century it held over two hundred thousand volumes. Many of those volumes were held in the temple of Athena, although not all of them were stored there because of space restrictions. Early in the second century C.E., a library was added to the temple of Asklepios, along with many other improvements to that temple. Library sciences progressed more quickly in Pergamum than in Egyptian Alexandria, including the use of parchment instead of papyrus as the material of texts and the use of the codex (i.e., a small book) instead of the scroll as the format of texts.

Letter Collection 3

The following is wholly fictional: the character Androneikos.

The following can be defended historically: the identity of Julius Quadratus and the occasion of the banquet in his honor; the status of Ephesus as a temple warden to the cult of the emperor in 89 C.E.; Domitian's funding of the refurbishment of the Ephesian temple of Artemis.

Gaius Antius Aulus Julius Quadratus was a wealthy and influential resident of Pergamum and a preeminent citizen of the Roman empire. Born in the early 50s as the son of Aulus, he was appointed to the senate by Emperor Vespasian in the early 70s and served from 81 to 84 as *legatus Augusti* to the cities of Cappadocia, Galatia, Phrygia, Lycaonia, Paphlagonia, and Armenia Minor. Having proved himself well in that position, he was seeking a position with even higher profile within the empire at the time of these letters. He was made proconsul of the province of Asia in 108 and later went on to establish regular games in Pergamum in honor of Jupiter Amicalis (Jupiter Philios) and the emperor Trajan.

Letter Collection 4

The following is speculative: the death of Peter and Paul in Nero's persecutions against the Christians (many scholars, for instance, date Paul's death earlier at ca. 62 C.E. instead of 64 C.E.).

The following can be defended historically: the appointment of Lysanius Paullus of Miletus as regional Asiarch; the description of water battles in the Flavian amphitheater; the description of Domitian's actions at the games near the Tiber River; the account of Nero's actions.

Letter Collection 5

The following can be defended historically: the widespread belief in the return of Nero (allusions to this widespread myth appear in Rev. 13:3; 17:8); the description of the Jewish revolt against Rome; the description of Sepphoris; the descriptions of Domitian's actions at a gladiatorial contest and beyond; the life and writings of Josephus (although see "A Note on Josephus" on page 192).

Letter Collection 6

The following is wholly fictional: the character Kalandion.

The report on the Pergamene games, while fictional, is based on reliable reconstructions of the way a gladiatorial day proceeded.

The following can be defended historically: the description of Nazareth; the description of John the Baptist; the description of Ephesian Christianity; the descriptions of the Dead Sea community (i.e., the Qumran sectarians) and the Essenes.

Letter Collection 7

The following is wholly fictional: the character Lycomedes.

The following can be defended historically: the description of the Pharisees; the character Earinus, Domitian's "favorite boy," raised in Pergamum.

Letter Collection 8

The following are wholly fictional (here and throughout): the characters Mama and Simon ben Joseph.

The following is speculative: Luke's involvement in compiling the final version of John's Gospel.

The following can be defended historically: the description of the Samaritans; the description of the Ephesian community of John.

Letter Collection 9

The following are wholly fictional: the characters Demetrius, Nouna, Glykeros, Kyrilos, Theodotos, and Tullia Spendousa.

The following can be defended historically: the significance of the term "Son of Man"; Roman consuls Octacilius Pollio and Claudius Charax (although dating from a few decades after the time of this narrative); the description of Pontius Pilate.

Letter Collection 10

The following can be defended historically: the description of peasant life.

Letter Collection 11

The following can be defended historically: the depiction of the influence of the imperial cult in Pergamum; the depiction of crucifixion; the outline of a few of Herod Antipas' achievements.

Letter Collection 12

The following are wholly fictional: the characters Galatia and her baby.

The following is speculative: Antioch as the provenance of Matthew's Gospel, although many scholars think this to be likely.

The description of the storm at sea, while fictional, is based on an actual account from the ancient world. Cf. Synesius, *Epistle* 4.160–64.

The following can be defended historically: the depiction of Syrian Antioch and the Christian communities there; Ignatius (although we know little of him from this time period); the importance of Jamnia for Judaism after the destruction of Jerusalem.

Letter Collection 13

The following can be defended historically: the influence of craft guilds and their strong connections to the imperial cult; the situation of John, the Christian prophet who wrote the Johannine apocalypse, Revelation (although it is speculative that he lived in Ephesus prior to his exile).

Letter Collection 14

The following are wholly fictional: the events described by Antonius, except for the slim details about the manner of Antipas' death, which, while speculative, are based on ancient tradition.

Editor's Postscript

The details given in the postscript can be defended historically.

A Note on Josephus

On pages 37, 44–45, and 56, I have taken the liberty of allowing Luke to cite works of Josephus that had not yet been published at the time of this correspondence. The Greek version of *War* was written by 79 C.E. and would have been available to Luke in 92 C.E. *Jewish Antiquities* was made public in 93–94 C.E.; *Life* was made public in 96 C.E. or so; *Against Apion* was made public in 97 C.E. or so.